Emery Brantham

JOHN A. NEWTON

Search for a Saint: Edward King

To Tony Stoneburner,
in gratitude,
John A. Newton.

27.xi.87.

London EPWORTH PRESS

7162 0281 6

Enquiries should be addressed to
The Methodist Publishing House
Wellington Road
Wimbledon
London SW19 8EU
Printed in Great Britain by
The Garden City Press Limited
Letchworth, Hertfordshire SG6 1JS

CONTENTS

Acknowledgements

Every effort has been made to trace owners of copyright. Any failure will, if possible, be made good in future editions. My thanks are due to the publishers of the following works for kindly allowing me to make one extended quotation from each of them:

J. G. Lockhart, *Cosmo Gordon Lang* (1949), Hodder & Stoughton.

Spiritual Letters of Edward King (1910), Mowbray & Co. Ltd.

Letters of C. S. Lewis (1966), Geoffrey Bles Ltd.

Sir Arthur Quiller-Couch, *Memories and Opinions* (1944), Cambridge University Press.

Oxford Dictionary of the Christian Church (art. 'Lincoln Judgement'), Oxford University Press.

Owen Chadwick, *The Mind of the Oxford Movement* (1960), A. & C. Black.

J. A. N.

TO MY MOTHER

... Altogether, I hope we are settling down to steady work, that is what we want, I think, in England now. We have learnt our lesson from abroad now, and we must remember to be grateful to them but now we must do it. We want to make people respect England. We have looked so much abroad during the last 25 years, but now we are trying to work and produce English books of all kinds, not only Theology, which are up to the mark; and we are beginning to do the same in Theology. We must work. And the same in personal life, we know the machinery now for Saint-making, and we have got the stuff, only we must work and make them. I want to see English saints made in the old way by suffering and labour and diligence in little things, and the exercise of unselfish, untiring love; quiet lives lived away in holes and corners and not known to the public while alive. I want to begin to write some 2d Lives of English Saints, with the names of counties and parishes and people we know, so that others may read them and try to do the same. Do let us try and rear a few quiet English Saints!

Edward King, 1875

CHAPTER ONE

'A few quiet English Saints'

The world needs saints, just as a plague-stricken city needs doctors.

Simone Weil

A new definition of sanctity—that is what we all, at this moment, stand more or less in need of.

Teilhard de Chardin

I am sorry you are not well, especially your throat, for just now it is most important to *read* LOUD and make as much *noise* as we can in the *service*, and not be creeping about in a mousey saintly way.

Edward King

TODAY the odour of sanctity seems to strike many nostrils as the smell of death. We live no doubt in a time of the breaking of nations. We live no less in a time of the breaking of images, institutions, traditions and ideas. Old forms of holiness, tried patterns of sanctity, no longer satisfy. So not only in the pruning of the Roman Kalendar, but in the practical devotion of many Christians, the saints go marching out.

Yet Charles Péguy, that politically conscious, radical Christian, is on record as saying, 'The only real disappointment in life is not to have been a saint'. It may often seem that the saints are like the literary classics : praised by all, but read by few, and understood by even less. Yet when a saint springs up in our own time and confronts us with the authentic grace of Christ, we stop and look and listen. 'The holiness of God,' as A. M. Allchin says, 'is always what we least expected. It works itself out in flesh and blood.'[1] When the flesh and blood is that of a Pope John XXIII or a Mother Teresa of Calcutta, even the world kindles and is surprised by joy. Indeed, one of the marks of the true saint is the power to appeal to those outside, at least as well

9

as to those inside, the Church; to Tom, Dick and Harry, as well as Peter, James and John.

Time certainly winnows the wheat from the chaff in this matter of sanctity. The man who is the object of our search in this book was recognized before his death in 1910 as one of God's saints. The last sixty-five years have amply confirmed that judgement. Because Edward King (1829–1910) was an Anglican, there has been no formal process of canonization. That is not the Anglican way of making saints. Even so, on 24 May 1935, the Church of England came as near to a deliberate canonization of one of her sons as at any time since the Reformation. One thousand nine hundred and thirty-five was a rich year for English saints. The Roman Church that year canonized Sir Thomas More, who had kept his integrity and lost his life under Henry VIII's brutal regime, as a martyr for the Catholic faith. King was in good company.

The Roman canonization of Thomas More and the Anglican celebration of Edward King were, formally, unconnected. There was no cross-representation of Churches at the two services, as would undoubtedly have happened if they had fallen in 1977— witness the impressively ecumenical gathering at Cardinal Heenan's funeral. In 1935, on the other hand, the Anglicans and Romans moved on parallel lines, which would meet only in an ecumenical infinity—or in heaven. Yet there was a link between the Roman and Anglican acts of saint-making. In the four hundred years of bitter Anglican-Roman controversy, a number of stock questions, the smooth round pebbles of debate, have been slung with some force at the brow of the Church of England. 'Where was your Church before the Reformation?' asks the Roman pointedly. 'And where was your face before you washed it this morning?' the Anglican parries, to make the score even. A more searching Roman question, to which a glib reply was hardly possible, was, 'Can your Church produce saints?' Part of the Anglican answer was given at Lincoln on 24 May 1935.

On that day a service to commemorate the fiftieth anniversary of the enthronement of Edward King as Bishop of Lincoln, the sixtieth of that line, was held in his cathedral church astride the hill on which the city stands. The Archbishop of Canterbury, Cosmo Gordon Lang, celebrated a Solemn Eucharist, and addressed the huge congregation on 'Edward King, Bishop and Saint'. The collect, epistle and gospel were specially prepared for the commemoration of Edward King, and have been used in the diocese ever since on March 8th, the anniversary of his death. That day the English Church had, formally but with exhilarating joy, recognized a modern saint.

What kind of man was being commemorated on that May day in 1935, in the cathedral where a quarter of a century before he had been buried in the sheltered cloister garth? This book will try to spell out an answer to that question. One of the most rewarding—and tantalizing—aspects of this search for Edward King is that it is still just possible to tap the first-hand stream of oral tradition from those who knew and talked with him. His sayings and sermon themes, texts and aphorisms were treasured, and still resonate in the memories of the Lincolnshire people. A Lincoln lady wrote to me in 1968: 'Your letter reminded me of a remark that was repeated to me more than once as a child, by an aunt of mine. . . . Bishop King decided to give up living at the Bishop's Palace out at Riseholme and to have his home in Lincoln because "It wasn't every poor parson who had half-a-crown for a cab out to Riseholme." These were the actual words that were repeated as his and always remained with me . . . I can remember as a child in Lincoln what an aura there was about the name and person of Bishop King and these words always stuck vividly in my mind.' Another lady, now in her eighties, writes of how as a schoolgirl she was scolded by her teacher for cutting across the cathedral green and through the church to get to school. King sought her out and 'told me that whenever I wanted to do so, I could cross the green, and I remember his words—"It is my cathedral and my green, and you can go on them every day, if you want to do so." Now when I go to Lincoln, I purposely walk right across the cathedral green, and remember his kindness and love to his little ones.' The stories and sayings are legion. Often simple, they nevertheless throw a shaft of light upon the essential man.

The same stream of personal reminiscence was tapped by Archbishop Lang, the preacher and celebrant at the great service of 1935. He lit up his sermon with an account of his own first meeting with Bishop King. Lang had been brought up a Presbyterian, but become an Anglican while a young Fellow of All Souls College, Oxford. His spiritual adviser, the historian Henry Wakeman, sent him off to Lincoln to be confirmed by King. Lang normally oozed self-confidence from every pore, but on this occasion was diffident and ill at ease. 'I went to Lincoln in a mood of unwonted shyness and nervousness. This mood was not relieved when I arrived. There was an Ordinands' Retreat going on and I was ushered straight into the room where the Bishop was supping with his Ordinands, and someone was reading to them in their silence. I had never seen men in cassocks before and I felt desperately like a fish out of water. But when I took my place beside him, the dear old Bishop seemed to discern my discomfort of mind and, putting his hand on my thigh, whispered to me: "They're not half as good as they look and I'm the naughtiest of them all." '[2]

That incident was of course trivial in itself. Yet it had stayed with Lang for over forty-five years, and it throws into relief King's humour and humanity, as well as his extraordinary gift for being able to see life through someone else's eyes.

It was in this enormous capacity for sympathy that two of his clergy who knew him best, Canon Randolph and Canon Townroe, saw the secret of his power. It was 'the power of sympathy linked with a special gift of natural attractiveness, together with the fact that he had real spiritual insight and understood the needs of the soul'. Then they develop the theme of King's attractiveness by drawing our gaze to the light in his face. The halo is not just an ecclesiastical convention. It tries to represent the 'brightness'—to use a favourite word of King's—or the 'aura', as the Lincoln lady put it, that radiates from the faces of those who most closely follow Christ. 'There was that beautiful, kindly, *luminous* face that you were obliged to look at if you were near it. You did not ask whether he was "handsome" or "good-looking", you simply thought or said "What a beautiful face!" And then, if you heard him talking, or if he spoke to you, you realized at once that it was not merely physical beauty which had drawn you to him. There was a singular beauty of character, of which the face was the outward and visible sign; and the most obvious, overwhelming, persistent trait of this beautiful character was its sympathy. You felt that he instinctively entered into your special case and your special interests.'[3]

As T. S. Gregory used to say, 'Most of us, when we see a man with a funny face coming down the street, just think to ourselves, "What a funny face that man's got"—and pass on without another thought; but if we were really Christians, we should know what it felt like to have a funny face.' By that test, certainly, Edward King was 'really Christian'.

There is good warrant to believe that no one would have been more surprised than King to hear himself called a saint. On 17 June 1909, in the year before he died, we find him at Boston for a sexcentenary celebration associated with a saint. The occasion was the six hundredth anniversary of the laying of the foundation stone of the tower of Boston's magnificent parish church, St Botolph's, or, more familiarly, 'Boston Stump'. John Betjeman acknowledges it as 'one of the largest, and in some respects the grandest, of all the parish churches of England'. Its great tower, crowned with its lantern, is the tallest in England, and dominates the fenland and the wide swinging skies of South Lincolnshire. At a splendid civic lunch in Shodfriars Hall, King was called on to respond to the Mayor's toast in honour of 'The Memory of St Botolph'. He confessed to 'a unique embarrassment', at having to 'return thanks for a saint of the seventh century, whose memory has been proposed at a public luncheon more than twelve hundred years after he was dead'. He thought that if St Botolph could have been present he would have been utterly astonished at the proceedings. 'I think it would startle the good saint if he really knew that his name was being proposed at a public luncheon by the Mayor of Boston—I really think that very likely he would run away. But no, that might be unworthy of the courage which belongs to the saints. I really think, to be serious, that the word "surprise" might be taken as the motto for the saints. He would have been surprised to see the outcome, so to say, of his life and teaching; he would have been surprised to have seen your magnificent Church, with that wonderful tower; he would have been surprised and delighted at the service which went on in that Church this morning; he would be surprised, when we know the humble and simple surroundings in which he lived this life here—yes, surprise is the true motto of saints.'[4]

Significantly, for Edward King, courage and surprise are the qualities he associates with the saints. The 'surprise of the saints' seems to have been compounded, in his mind, of humility and that unselfconscious goodness which not only does not think more highly of itself than it ought to think, but hardly considers itself at all : '. . . surprise is the true motto of saints. Good people do not know what they are doing. Good people, as a rule, differ from us ordinary people. Most of us ordinary people know how to be a great deal better than we are, but really good people are generally a great deal better than they know how to be; they are not conscious at all of being what they are. They are simply what they are, good people, and so they are surprised when the result of their lives at all comes out into view.' One wonders how many of those present, hearing King put himself among the 'ordinary people' rather than the 'good people', realized the living proof he was unconsciously giving that the genuine saints 'are not conscious at all of being what they are'. He went on to speak of 'the parable of the Gospel of the last day', the sheep and the goats, the parable of the great surprise in St Matthew, chapter 25. 'Surely the good saints were surprised to find that they had been so good. . . . At the last day the saints would be surprised that they had been made by God's grace what they had been made. I don't know what the Saint would wish me to say, but I feel sure of this that he, being the good man that he was—he may have been different in appearance—in different ages the saints have sometimes had more adornment on their clothes and things of that sort, possibly a little more dirt upon their hands sometimes— but it is not the clean hands that make the saint, it is the clean heart . . . (The saints) are all, as it were, like beads that may be of different colours, may be of a different shape, may be of a different mercantile value according to the markets of this world, but they are all strung upon one golden thread, the golden thread of love—love of God and love of man.'[5]

Courage, surprise ('What, *me*? A *saint*?'), purity of heart, love of God and man : these for King make up the hall-mark of sanctity. These are virtues which spring from a kind of *ecstasy*, a going out of oneself, bravely, self-forgetfully, in love to the other. 'Purity of heart', as Kierkegaard reminds us, 'is to will one thing.' The saints are those who concentrate on that 'one thing', the one thing needful, the true love of God and man. They are so absorbed, rapt, caught up in this one pursuit, that they have no time for self. In that self-oblivion lies their sanctity.

This patient absorption has about it something of the dedication of the artist or the craftsman. Where the craftsman or artist is also a lover of God and man, he may approximate even more strikingly to the saint. So Father Peter Levi, S. J., preaching at a Solemn Requiem for David Jones, the Catholic poet, painter, sculptor, on 13 December 1974, could say of him : 'He worked like a hermit in a cave but a very sociable hermit. He rejoiced in tiny luxuries, he loved his friends, he turned his face to the light. He was so patient that his face became saint-like and David smiling transfigures every memory of him.'[6] He worked . . . rejoiced . . . loved . . . and turned his face to the light. So did King; and the light was reflected in his 'radiant and joyous face'.[7] As Henry Scott Holland recalled so vividly, 'It was light that he carried with him, light that shone through him, light that flowed from him. The room was lit into which he entered. It was as if we had fallen under a streak of sunlight that flickered, and danced, and laughed, and turned all to colour and gold. Those eyes of his were an illumination. Even to recall him for an instant in the bare memory was enough to set all the day alive and glittering.'[8]

We catch a second glimpse of King's view of a saint in the two sermons he preached on St Hugh of Avalon, who was

Bishop of Lincoln from 1186 to 1200. Hugh, the Burgundian nobleman who became a Carthusian monk, is the other great saint to hold the see of Lincoln. In the diocese, the names of Hugh of Avalon and Edward King are naturally bracketed together. Cecilia Ady records a verger's reply to a visitor's enquiry about the great bronze statue of King in the south transept of Lincoln cathedral : 'He was a very great saint, as great a saint as St Hugh !'[9] There is a striking coalescence of the two saints in the reredos of the church of St Peter-at-Gowts, in Lincoln High Street, where the figure of St Hugh wears the face of Edward King.

In his sermon of 1900, for the seven hundredth anniversary of Hugh's death, King picked out 'the principal features of his character which made him the saintly man he was'.[10] He lists them as : the holiness of his youth; his loving devotion to his father—'He had none of the spirit of Corban which would make the formal duties of religion an excuse for neglecting the natural duties of home ties . . . '; his lifelong self-discipline, although 'he did not require others to take so hard a rule as he adopted for himself'; his courage and fearless sense of justice; his consummate tact, which embraced 'good taste, good feeling, good sense, much insight, a consideration for the feelings of others'; his vivid faith and passionate devotion to the scriptures; his prolonged meditation and prayer; and 'a singular sympathy, and tenderness towards the young, and the poor, and the sick, and the dying and the dead'.[11]

A year later, preaching on the Feast of St Hugh, on 17 November 1901, he interpreted Psalm 103:20 not only of the angels, but also of the saints as those who '*do* God's Will' and '*listen* for the voice of His words'.[12] Typically, he did not leave this ideal at the level of lofty—and eminently forgettable—generalization. He brought it down to earth, and converted it into the small change of daily living, asking himself and his hearers : 'Am I conscious as it were of hearing voices that call me to do something that I leave undone, something perhaps quite simple in the daily duties of home life; to pay more attention to the bodily wants of some sick or aged member of the family; to pay more attention to the religious education of the children; to do my daily work better, to be less selfish, and to think more of a neighbour's troubles and wants; to take a larger share in spreading the good news of the Gospel at home or even abroad? This is the way to imitate the *hearkening* of the Angels and the Saints. . . .'[13]

It was Brother Lawrence's secret, of course: 'To do little things, for the love of God.' In King's words, 'the ladder of the saints', when they responded to the call to 'come up higher', was 'by little steps, by doing daily duties better, by loving God and loving our neighbour'. As he had written to a young ordinand over a quarter of a century before, in 1874: 'Get a steady habit of self-control, so as to do the Divine Will in little daily duties—this is the inner armour of the saints.'[14] Dr Pusey, King's friend and colleague at Christ Church, Oxford, held a very similar view: 'Holiness consists not in doing uncommon things, but in doing common things in an uncommon way.'[15]

The ladder of the saints, the scale of perfection, the ascending of the hill of the Lord: these variations on a theme are common in the literature of spirituality. John Henry Newman has his own inimitable treatment of the 'ladder', which it is interesting to compare with King's. Newman turns the theme into an awful warning along the lines of 'the higher they come, the harder they fall'. 'No paradox is truer than this,' he insists, 'that the higher we are in holiness, the more we are in danger of going wrong. I have been accustomed to compare the ascent to perfection to the mounting of a higher ladder. As the climber gets higher the ladder dances under him—behold the state of the soul mounting towards heaven. . . . This is why saints are so few—they drop off as they get more likely to be saints.'[16] King's emphasis is different, more hopeful and encouraging. He stresses not the ladder tottering under the pressure of toiling feet, but the call from above which elicits a patient, steady obedience. He knows well enough that the saints are fallible, but draws encouragement rather than admonition from the fact: 'The lives of the saints are recorded for our edification, to lift us up above the average level with which the world is generally content. Their perfections are to be to us examples of the heights to which man with God can reach; and yet it is often the imperfections and faults of the saints which seem to help us most, to give us comfort, to save us from despair, proving to us that God can pardon and love again. The concluding record of David's sin is wonderfully rapid—"and she bare a son, and he called his name Solomon, *and the Lord loved him*".[17]

King understood deeply, and exemplified, the humanity of the saints. He knew the dangers of *ersatz* spirituality, of spiritual pride, of trying to force growth in goodness like rhubarb under a bucket, of claiming instant holiness. All these were abhorrent to him. What he looked for, like the countryman he was, was a quiet, steady growth in goodness. What we need, he would say, is 'a few quiet English saints'. One of his students, in King's days as a theological college principal, had scruples about going shooting in the vacation. Was it a proper relaxation for an intending parson? Would he be soiling his cloth? In our day, when parsons have been known to drive steam-engines at rallies and referee women's wrestling, it would seem to be a non-question. It was not so in Victorian England, and King weighed the question carefully. In his reply, he urged the man to go ahead and shoot, adding, 'I am not saying all this out of false kindness, because, I think, it is telling you to do what you like (I love you too truly for that), but because I do value so highly a natural growth in holiness, a humble grateful acceptance of the circumstances God has provided for each of us, and I dread the unnatural, forced, cramped ecclesiastical holiness, which is so much more quickly produced, but is so human and so poor.'[18]

I think King might have found some of our twentieth-century Christian talk about 'worldly holiness' little more than religious cant—telling people out of false kindness to do what they like to do and are all too adept at doing already. But the wedding of the worldly—i.e. the creaturely, commonplace, homely—and the holy, *that* he would have understood and endorsed; and not as a theorist, but as one who incarnated it.

CHAPTER TWO

The Oriel Undergraduate

King is a royal fellow.   *Charles Marriott*

E DWARD K ING, or 'little Ted' as his mother called him
in the first weeks of his life, was born in London on 29
December 1829. His father, Walker King, was a clergyman
and later Archdeacon of Rochester. His mother, Anne
Heberden, was the daughter of a distinguished London doctor,
William Heberden of Pall Mall. Mrs King moved into London
for her confinement so as to be near her father, though the
family lived in Kent, where Walker King was Rector of Stone,
and ministered in the splendid thirteenth-century parish church
of St Mary.

Edward, the second son, was privately baptized by his father
in the house of his birth, 8 St James's Place, Piccadilly. He was
born into a world which, for most of his fellow-countrymen, was
cold and hard and bitter. It was the world of the 'Two Nations',
even though Disraeli had not yet coined the phrase. It was a
world of rick-burnings by desperate farm-workers; of savage
rioting in favour of Parliamentary Reform; of labourers found
dead of starvation under the hedgerows; of cholera, typhus and
dysentery. A couple of months before King's birth, George
Stephenson's 'Rocket' had won the Liverpool and Manchester
railway competition. It was not fifteen years since the Napole-
onic Wars had ended, bringing inflation and depression in their
wake. Over forty years later, Edward King would still recall
'the great battle, the talk of our childhood—the battle of
Waterloo', which, though 'fought on . . . a very small spot . . .
gave England and Europe peace'.[1] It was also the era of 'the
Church in danger', in danger, so it seemed, of expropriation
from Whigs, reformers, radicals and revolutionaries, who had
all drunk. more or less deeply, from the cup of 1789. The

Church was, of course, the Church of England, in whose service King was born, lived and died.

King's life (1829–1910) spanned the whole of the Victorian period, and he was a Victorian of the Victorians. If that makes him seem an ancient rather than a modern to us, then we have hardly begun to understand the nature of the epoch in which the Great Queen ruled. Increasingly we can see the nineteenth century as the seed-bed of so many of our major problems today. It was the century of Darwin, Marx and Freud; of massive developments in industry and urbanization; of the revolution in transport wrought by the railways; of triumphant and expanding capitalism; of colonial and imperial rivalry in the scramble for Africa.

Edward King was born to live through a tempestuous era. What were his resources as he set out on his life's journey? Physically, it seemed, not great. He was a delicate child, and his private baptism prefigured a private childhood and a sheltered early life. Partly from anxiety over his health, his parents never sent him away to school, as they sent his elder brother, Walker, but educated him at home. He enjoyed a close and happy family life with his nine brothers and sisters, and treasured it always. He was to be utterly devoted to his mother, who for the last twenty years of her life made her home with him.

Archdeacon Walker King's means allowed him to decline the rectory attached to St Mary's, a damp unhealthy house, and to live instead at Stone Park, a spacious pleasant mansion of his own. Today the parish of Stone, unable to support its own incumbent, is grouped with St Peter, Oare, and St Mary the Virgin, Luddenham, to form one enlarged cure. In 1830, it supported a curate as well as the rector, both of whom were to play a major part in Edward's schooling. It was his mother who taught him his catechism,[2] but his father gave him his initial schooling; the curate, John Day, then took him on as an older pupil. The religious instruction he received at home no doubt served as a 'remote preparation' when the time came for him to be confirmed. There was certainly no immediate or specific preparation, and in the casualness of approach we are reminded that the Oxford Movement had not yet begun to revolutionize the life and practice of the Church of England. His father simply asked him one day if he knew his catechism, found he did, and without more ado packed him off on horseback to be confirmed by Archbishop Howley at Foot's Cray near by.[3] When Edward came home, though he was a good and keen dancer, he decided not to join the rest of the family at the dancing to which they were going that evening, but to stay quietly at home. His mother understood completely and did not press him. Evidently lack of formal preparation did not mean for him a superficial approach to the vows he had made that day. Did he remember the day of his own confirmation, and its lack of formality, when years later a country clergyman got on his high horse and complained to King as bishop about the spiritual obtuseness of one of the young farm lads among his would-be new communicants? 'For example, my Lord,' he said, 'there is one lad with whom I had taken much trouble, and I hoped an influence for good was getting a lodgement in the boy's heart. But, imagine my distress when I asked what he had done in the way of preparation for his early Communion at Easter, and all he said was, "I's cleaned my boots, and put 'em under the bed." It is sad, indeed!' To which King replied gently, 'Well, dear friend, and don't you think the angels would rejoice to see them there?'[4]

Edward was evidently drawn to his tutor, young Mr Day, for when Day left his curacy at Stone, first for Flintshire and then to become the vicar of Ellesmere near Oswestry in Shropshire, King went with him. At Ellesmere he became a kind of lay assistant to the vicar, quite undeterred by the fact that he was a species of church worker unknown to the canon law of the Anglican Church. He led a men's Bible Class, sang in the choir, and made himself generally useful in the parish. When he left Ellesmere for Oxford at the age of eighteen, he took with him an inscribed Prayer Book, 'presented by the Choir of Ellesmere, in token of their affectionate regard and grateful remembrance, July 19th, 1848'. Less tangibly, he took to Oxford two other benefits from his time at Ellesmere. First, he had gained a wider experience of the life and ministry of the Church, in his first taste of work away from home. Secondly, in working with John Day, he had made his first direct contact with the Tractarian Movement. Day was one of the younger generation of clergy, who had been fired by the new High Churchmanship which had been emanating from Oxford since the early 1830s. His time at Brasenose College from 1830 to 1834 had seen the start of the Oxford Movement, and as vicar of Ellesmere from 1846 to his death in 1864, he tried to translate the Movement's ideals into parochial practice, as John Keble had done so notably at Hursley.

Edward King could hardly have chosen a more tumultuous year to begin his studies at Oriel College than 1848. The Year of Revolutions saw upheavals in Paris, Berlin, Vienna, Milan, Cracow, Prague; and the monster petition of the Chartists in London. It was the year of the *Communist Manifesto*, a trickle of a stream that would later cleave the rocks. In matters of religion the times were no less critical. In 1848, the Oxford historian J. A. Froude, who had been caught up by Newman into the High Church movement, registered his loss of Christian conviction in his *Nemesis of Faith*. (Newman's own brother, Frank, was to chart a similar course in his spiritual autobiography, published two years later, *Phases of Faith*.) Frederic Harrison went up to Wadham College in 1848 as a 'neo-Catholic', and left college as a convinced Positivist and devout believer in 'the religion of humanity'.

Even Oriel, the stronghold of Tractarianism, the college of Newman, Keble, Pusey, Hurrell Froude, Robert Wilberforce, was being permeated by the new temper of scepticism, doubt, unbelief. There were still staunch Tractarians among the Fellows of the College—J. W. Burgon, Charles Marriott, R. W. Church—all gifted and devoted men. Yet Newman's defection to Rome in 1845 had shaken Oxford and Oriel to the core, and left the High Church party shattered and demoralized. It took all the efforts of Pusey and Marriott to rally the broken ranks. When the young King came up to Oriel in 1848, the fall-out from the explosion had still not settled. In Oxford there was a sharp reaction from Evangelicals and Liberals against religious controversy such as the Tractarians had provoked. There were many who, in Dean Tuckwell's words, 'thought that Humanism and Science might reassert themselves as subject matter of education against the polemic which had for fifteen years forced Oxford back into the barren word-war of the seventeenth century'.[5] As some in the twentieth century have hailed the passing of Karl Barth's domination of the theological scene as 'the end of the great blight', so many in the Oxford of 1848 rejoiced that the spell woven by John Henry Newman had been broken.

In point of fact, the accounts of the collapse of the Oxford Movement were, as Mark Twain used to say of the newspaper reports of his own decease, 'greatly exaggerated'. Yet there is no doubt that Newman's departure for Rome in 1845 was a watershed. His going ushered in a new and intense time of troubles for High Church Anglicans, who for a while could do little more than keep their heads down while the hurricane swept over them. The gale of reaction had still not blown itself out by 1848, certainly not in Oriel, where the Provost, Edward Hawkins, was a fierce anti-Tractarian, bent on making the college once more a place fit for Churchmen to live in. Oriel in 1848 was clearly not exactly the Promised Land for a young freshman like King who was drawn to the Tractarian position.

Two Fellows of Oriel reflect the ferment of faith in the Oxford of the late 1840s, and show how hard it was to remain a High Anglican after 1845. With Newman gone, it was as though a great tide had gone out. Some, like Henry Coleridge, a Fellow of Oriel 1845–52, took the same tide and went to Rome, where he became a prominent Jesuit and rector of the church in Farm Street. Others moved in the opposite direction, and took the path of Frank Newman or Mark Pattison, towards agnosticism or unbelief. Arthur Hugh Clough resigned his fellowship at Oriel in the very year King entered college, because of growing religious doubts. In 1848, Coleridge was already mentally on the move from Canterbury to Rome, while Clough was becoming the sad, ironical agnostic his poems reveal.

When King entered Oriel as an eighteen-year-old under-

23

graduate he soon found that the High Churchmen were under a cloud, and that to profess and practise Catholic Anglicanism was to be a sign that is spoken against. King had at Oriel a small taste of that opposition to his churchmanship which was to follow him, at times with great virulence, throughout his life. Whatever people thought of King as a Christian man, there is no doubt that for most of his life he was an intensely controversial figure. Is that so surprising? Does it strike a jarring note that a preacher whose favourite text was, 'Thy gentleness hath made me great', should have known so much of the dust of combat? If so, where does the incongruity lie? Surely not in the mere fact of engaging in controversy, for the Lord himself has a controversy with his people, and Jesus was so often drawn into argument that his parables have been seen as 'words of conflict', sinews of war in the battle continually raging about him.

It is arguable that the great saints are always controversial. We can make them uncontroversial only by clipping their wings and cutting them down to our own Lilliputian size. A St Teresa of Avila or a St Bernard of Clairvaux is an uncomfortable and disturbing person, sharpening issues, piercing through masks of unreality, laying bare the truth, like the sharp-edged sword of the Word of God. Even the gentle saints—St Francis de Sales, St Philip Neri, John Keble, St Aelred of Rievaulx—have a streak of toughness and tenacity in them. The life of Mother Teresa of Calcutta may be full of sweetness and light, but it is also tempered steel. The saints, almost by definition, are signs that are spoken against. They speak not only of the goodness of God, but of the wrath of the Lamb. In Charles Wesley's words,

> Jesus, the meek, the angry Lamb,
> A Lion is in fight.

So are many of his closest followers. The quiet anger of the meek is a terrible thing. Just because their zeal for righteousness is largely undeflected by our own ceaseless self-reference, they are formidable warriors in the cause of truth. Gentleness is not weakness, but restrained strength.

'Beware when all men speak well of you', was not a warning King often needed to hear. Yet merely to rouse widespread opposition is obviously no guarantee of sanctity, or every crank in Christendom might expect canonization. How far did King draw resentment upon himself by personal abrasiveness or by extreme views immoderately expressed? As a Catholic Anglican in the nineteenth century, he was inevitably caught in the cross-fire of religious party strife. Catholics of the Roman obedience could not stomach his Anglicanism. His fellow-Anglicans who were either Evangelicals or Broad Church Liberals detested his Catholicism as a betrayal of the Reformation. The question was not *whether* King would maintain his Tractarian position in face of opposition, but *how*. Would he hold on to his faith, but only at the price of becoming intense, shrill, fanatical? Would he turn into a rigid party man? If he maintained his High Anglican churchmanship, would he also be capable of growth and development, so as to embrace a new age within his catholicity? Or would he get inside the *laager* of Boer wagons with Pusey, Liddon and Burgon, and die in the last ditch?

Oriel gave King's Catholicism the first of many testings. (He can hardly be called a full-blooded Tractarian at this stage, but his home and John Day had tended to make him an unsophisticated High Churchman.) The challenge was not as dramatic as later ones he faced, but it was significant, both because it was the first, and because he met it at such an impressionable age. With his background of family and faith, King was bound to find the Oxford of 1848 something of a slap in the face. It was the Oxford of Tom Brown and Verdant Green, and its undergraduate life could be as randy and bawdy as it had been in the High Middle Ages. King had had a sheltered upbringing in a devout home. He had not been through the mill of public school. Pious and inexperienced, he might have seemed easy meat for the young bucks who presided over the low life of the university, on whom such learning as they had acquired sat with all the incongruity of a silk hat on a Bradford millionaire. He was no doubt as shockable as the boy from a godly home going up to university today, and finding that the

Student's Handbook, in its brash, confident way, favours him with full details of contraceptive and family planning facilities. It may not actually list the brothels, but the inference will be clear enough that in the contemporary very 'open' university morally anything goes. If, on the other hand, the student has the moral stamina to resist the downdrag, he may easily become a pious prig, retreating either into private soul-culture or into a tight group of the elect and 'unco' guid'.

How did King in fact make out? It seems clear he maintained his standards and kept his integrity. He is said to have been once invited to a college 'wine'—something akin to the modern 'cheese and wine' party—when a guest began to sing a bawdy song. King simply left the 'wine' and never went to one again.[6] Whether or not this account is well-based, it is certainly in line with the advice King was to give in 1863 to a young friend of his who had just begun his course at Culham Teacher Training College. King wrote to him :

'And so now you are really at College !

'I hardly know what to say to you. However, go on in your old way. Don't be in a hurry to change for new ways, which others would persuade you are better or more independent, or more telling in the world. Beware of smart dealing, swaggering, loud talking, showing off your knowledge, thinking yourself a *great government man*!! etc. All these things are simply *poor*. Pray don't be tempted by them, my dearest C——. You must be careful at first with whom you make friends. There are no doubt some very nice fellows, but there are sure to be some of both sorts, and the bad ones are generally the first to make friends. . . .

'. . . I need not add that you must keep away from all real harm. Simply get out of the way of all bad conversation; go away from it; it is poison and contemptible. Don't stand it, but leave the fellows.'[7] Well, that is clear enough advice. It takes John Wesley's point that 'vice never loses its nature by becoming popular'. It has about it the decisiveness of the New Testament, 'If your eye offend you, pluck it out . . .' It does not underestimate the power of the enemy.

Yet that advice, surely, could make a man a pious prig? It might, certainly, depending on how he took it. King himself, interestingly, was never regarded as a prig at Oriel. A college contemporary of his left it on record : 'I can only remember being greatly impressed by the singularly high estimation in which his character was held by all sorts and conditions of men.'[8] Men do not respect a prig, and there is nothing like student irreverence for puncturing the balloon of pomposity. It would seem that the Oriel undergraduates endorsed Charles Marriott's judgement : 'King is a royal fellow.' King in fact not only worked at his books and maintained his religious discipline, but also 'ate hearty' at the full banquet of Oxford life. Before he went up to Oriel he had been keen on dancing, riding, fishing, and swimming. At Oxford he rowed on the river and enjoyed walking.

Yet he kept the ordered priorities of his life. A friend recalled : 'I have had many a pleasant afternoon's walk with Edward King, but he would never consent to go with you unless you promised to be back by Chapel-time, which was 4.30.'[9] King was later to advise his young friend at Culham College : 'Keep to your services. The Holy Communion every Sunday I think you may do, and the rest as often as you can. A few years of discipline makes the rest of life much easier.'[10] His own discipline of devotion included daily attendance at College Chapel and observance of the days marked for fasting in the Prayer Book. To an Oxford man who put himself under his direction, King later wrote : 'My way at Oxford of observing Friday was to keep out of Hall, and have tea in my own rooms.'[11] In other words, he took no college meals, and only one light meal on his own.

Quiet, strict devotion was the Tractarian ideal, and King was beginning to acquire it. The Provost of Oriel, Edward Hawkins, who kept up a genial personal interest in all his undergraduates, duly took note. Tractarianism to Hawkins was a red rag to a bull. An old-fashioned High Churchman himself, he had had to endure the mortification of seeing his brightest younger fellows become infected with 'Newmania'. There was no doubt a glint in his eye when Edward King came before him at the end of his first term for 'Collections', the formal interview given to each junior member of the college. Hawkins eyed him askance and warned him stiffly, 'I observe, Mr King, that you have never missed a single chapel, morning or evening, during the whole term. I must warn you, Mr King, that even too regular attendance at chapel may degenerate into formalism.'[12] To be fair to Hawkins—'dry and unbending' as Newman calls him—it was not only would-be Tractarians who felt the rap of his cane across their knuckles. He was a cool, rational Churchman of the old 'high and dry' school, who could no more stomach any brand of extreme or eccentric religion than he could tolerate an undergraduate who smelt of tobacco. One of his undergraduates, an ardent Evangelical, began to preach freelance in the slum district of St Ebbe's. When Hawkins stamped on his efforts, the man protested, 'But, sir, if the Lord who commanded me to preach, came suddenly to judgement *now*, what should I do?' With the full assurance of an Oxford Head of House, Hawkins refused to be browbeaten by eschatology: 'I will take the whole responsibility of that upon myself.'[13]

How did King react to the cold anti-Tractarian wind blowing through Oxford in the late 1840s, a wind that was especially icy in the quadrangles of Oriel? He seems to have followed the advice he was later to give to many who sought his spiritual direction: 'Go quietly and bravely on.' There is no sign that the Provost's rather acidulated remark had any effect on his pattern of devotion. His positive reaction seems to have been to look more and more to the example of the men of the Oxford Movement ('the late unhappy movement', as Provost Hawkins called it in his sermons), in his own college.

The great days of Tractarian Oriel had clearly gone; yet Burgon, Marriott and Church among the fellows kept the flame burning, and each of them left his mark on King. Burgon was his tutor and later recommended him to Bishop ('Soapy Sam') Wilberforce for a curacy in the Diocese of Oxford.[14] Church's learning and devotion so impressed King that, half a century later, as Bishop of Lincoln, he still kept a photograph of Church on his desk. Of the three High Church Fellows, however, it was Charles Marriott whose life left the most indelible impress on King.

It so happens that both Burgon and Church have left on record their personal recollections of Marriott, Burgon as one of his *Lives of Twelve Good Men* (1888) and Dean Church in his classic account of *The Oxford Movement: Twelve Years 1833–1845* (1891). Together they give an extraordinarily vivid portrait of Marriott, who was clearly one of the great Oxford characters of his day : eccentric, shy, outlandish in dress, and yet unmistakably a saint. His appearance was frankly grotesque. He dressed like a beggar, wore a veil over his eyes in summer and a dark-green shade in winter, swathed a black scarf round his neck, and draped himself in 'a cloak made of two old M.A. gowns unequally yoked together'.[15] His sudden appearance at night terrified small boys and college porters, and no wonder. Yet he dressed in this tatterdemalion fashion so as to be able to give away every possible penny to the needy. Though one of the finest patristic scholars in Oxford, he gave not only his money but his time unstintingly in pastoral care and in the service of the poor. Church testifies : '... there was no claimant on his purse or his interest who was too strange for his sympathy—raw freshmen, bores of every kind, broken-down tradesmen, old women, distressed foreigners, converted Jews, all the odd and helpless wanderers from beaten ways, were to be heard of at Marriott's rooms.'[16]

Marriott, by his pastoral sympathy and his deep spirituality, made a permanent mark on King, who freely acknowledged in later life, 'If I have any good in me, I owe it to Charles Marriott. He was the most Gospel-like man I have ever met.'[17] Nearly half a century after he first met Marriott at Oriel, King confessed to the assembled bishops of the Lambeth Conference of 1897 that he had found Marriott simply Christ-like : 'Our aim, then, is to be Christ-like Christians. This endeavour to set the life of Christ before ourselves as a practical guide of life, as a pattern for the formation of our own character, was first definitely brought home to me by the example of Charles

Marriott. When Constantine Prichard wrote his little "Commentary on the Epistle to the Romans" he dedicated it to the memory of Charles Marriott. Mr Prichard was, as some will remember, a Fellow of Balliol, and therefore a scholar, and accustomed to the accurate use of words, and yet his dedication ran thus: "To the memory of Charles Marriott, whose noble life was a living commentary on the Four Gospels." [18]

In Marriott King saw all the great virtues of Tractarianism: its discipline, its holiness, its concern for the poor. He saw all these, too, in Dr Pusey, whom he never ceased to admire, and who gave his name ('Puseyism') to the movement when the epidemic of 'Newmania' had burnt itself out. Another quality, however, King found in Marriott which was hard to discern in Pusey: joy. For Pusey, religion was real, religion was earnest. It was also overspread with a rather thick layer of gloom. With Marriott, however, cheerfulness was for ever breaking in. Even on his death-bed, he could not resist a joke; and a friend who visited him found, 'his half-paralysed brain was still active and his sense of fun acute. A new lodging house, ugly, comfortless, uninviting, had been built close by; the owner asked John Marriott' (Charles' brother) 'what he should call it. Charles suggested the *Redan*— it was the time of our repulse before Sebastopol—"because it would never be taken".' [19]

As well as joy, Marriott had a sober confidence that, despite the disaster of Newman's leaving the Movement in 1845, it was possible to look forward not merely with courage—Pusey had plenty of that—but with hope. There was opposition, it was true, and one must reckon seriously with that; but not too seriously, since, as Julian of Norwich's optimism of grace would have it, 'All shall be well, and all manner of thing shall be well'. In the course of a long life, Edward King was to demonstrate the same faith. It would be rash to say that he found it at Oriel. It would be even more rash to deny the powerful influence of Marriott of Oriel in its strengthening and confirmation.

CHAPTER THREE

Cuddesdon

> I regarded the establishment of Cuddesdon College as
> a scheme for unprotestantising the clergy as far as the
> influence of such an institution could reach.
>
> *C. P. Golightly*

> I have a strong conviction that Cuddesdon College is
> doing God's work for men's souls mightily.
>
> *Bishop Samuel Wilberforce*

On a May afternoon in 1921, C. S. Lewis, then an undergraduate at University College, Oxford, left his books and his
desk to go for a cycle ride. He and a friend, 'after stopping for
a drink at Garsington, . . . rode along the top of a long hill,
where you look down into a good, woody English valley with
the Chilterns, rather sleek and chalky . . . on the horizon. It was
a grey day, with clouds in muddled perspective all round. Just
as the first drops of rain began to fall, we found a young man
looking as if he was going to be hanged, crossing a field. He
turned out to be one Smith of Univ., who is now gone down
and is incarcerated at a High Church Theological Seminary in
the neighbouring village of Cuddesdon. "He would have liked
to ask us into tea, but couldn't—indeed oughtn't to be talking
to us—because they were having a *quiet day!*" Ye gods; a lot
of young men shut up together, all thinking about their souls!
Isn't it awful? After this it was quite fresh and lively to investigate an old windmill near Wheatley. . . .'[1]

Poor 'Smith of Univ.',—to be caught by the sharp eye and
deft pen of the young Lewis, and pinned down like a butterfly
with his hangdog expression and furtive conversation, shattering
the silence of a Cuddesdon quiet day. Yet it is fair to say,
perhaps, that this letter tells us as much about Lewis as it does
about Cuddesdon: Lewis, the Ulster Protestant turned atheist,

and not yet re-converted to Christianity, to whom any 'High Church Theological Seminary' inevitably spelt incarceration. Lewis could hardly have known it, but attacks on Cuddesdon as a High Church seminary had a long pedigree. The College was founded for clergy training in 1854 by Bishop Samuel Wilberforce, in whose diocese of Oxford it stood. It had been open barely three years when a formidable Oxford clergyman, the Revd Charles Portales Golightly, launched a broadside against its alleged Romanizing tendencies, in the pages of the *Quarterly Review* for January 1858. Golightly was quick and rash, but a man of genuine integrity. He could bring some heavy artillery to bear against Cuddesdon, for he was possessed of a sharp mind, a ready pen, and some not inconsiderable private means.

Bishop Wilberforce appointed Edward King Chaplain of Cuddesdon in the Michaelmas of 1858, so that King walked straight into the hornets' nest Golightly had stirred up. Wilberforce knew and trusted King, whom he had previously ordained to a curacy at Wheatley, next door to Cuddesdon. King joined a small staff at the College, comprising Principal, Vice-Principal, and Chaplain. The man who had done most to gain Cuddesdon a reputation for Romanism was the gifted Vice-Principal, Henry Parry Liddon. Liddon was to become one of the great preachers of the nineteenth century, a Canon of St Paul's who was to hold the great congregation beneath the Dome in the hollow of his hand. In 1858 he was twenty-nine years old, handsome, learned, eloquent, charming—and an utterly uncompromising High Churchman. The future Professor of Biblical Exegesis at Oxford and learned biographer of Pusey had immense personal gifts, but tact, discretion, and pastoral sense were not high among them. He was a rigorist, a hard-liner, extreme and unbending in both theology and churchmanship. For most of his life men were to say that he should have been a bishop. As a diocesan he would certainly have been a strong leader of the troops. Yet he had a fatal flaw, and one can finally see him only as a bishop *manqué*. The flaw is pinpointed by a letter from Mr Gladstone to Lord Selborne, written in 1884, when Liddon was still a strong theoretical contender for a bishopric.

Gladstone is speaking of the criteria he made use of when choosing men to be bishops : 'There is one [qualification] which I peculiarly look for, . . . I call it the spirit of government—the spirit of tolerance and just and kindly allowance . . . I dread being responsible for any appointment which will undermine or rend the Church . . .'[2] It was Liddon's marked lack of 'the spirit of tolerance and just and kindly allowance' that was at the root of the troubled situation at Cuddesdon into which King now entered.

At Cuddesdon in 1858, as at Oriel ten years earlier, King found himself facing opposition on account of his High Church-manship. This time the attacks came from outside the college, not from within. Yet it was the same anti-Tractarian resentment from men who saw the High Church party as a fifth column of popery within the Established Church, as traitors within the gates. It will be as well now to scrutinize the place where the traitors were alleged to lurk, and ask what sort of college Cuddesdon was. Cuddesdon was the brain-child of Bishop Samuel Wilberforce, built just across the road from his episcopal palace. Palace and college still stand today, astride the road in the quiet village of Cuddesdon, which lies a mile or two—and several centuries—away from the Cowley motor works.

Samuel Wilberforce was a dynamo, a man of enormous energy and vision, who was determined to drag the Church of England—or at least the Oxford Diocese—kicking and struggling into the nineteenth century. A superb organizer, he remodelled the episcopate as surely as Cromwell remodelled the Parliamentary Army. He has been unfortunately stereotyped as 'Soapy Sam', and fixed for ever, like a fly in amber, in the incident of his clash with Huxley over the Darwinian theory. Readers of David Newsome's poignant study of Manning and the Wilberforces, *The Parting of Friends,* may well find a new appreciation of this gifted and devoted man.

Wilberforce founded Cuddesdon as part of a far-reaching programme of modernization for his diocese. The college would not only supply clergy for the Oxford Diocese, but would drastically improve the quality of their training. What was the matter, many contemporaries asked, with the training they were getting before these new-fangled theological colleges were thought of? Were not the universities precisely intended to produce parish clergy, scholars and gentlemen, each of whom, after training as curate to an experienced parish priest, should be perfectly adequate for the cure of souls? The universities were supposed to do just that, and as late as 1840 some fifty per cent of all men studying at Oxford and Cambridge were doing so with a view to being ordained. The question was : were the universities any longer adequate for the task of equipping men, devotionally, pastorally, theologically, for the work of the ministry? Wilberforce was quite clear in his own mind that they were not. At the Cuddesdon stone-laying, he opened his mind : 'Far be it from me to say anything in disparagement of our Universities, yet they do not meet the case. They may be all very well for those who wish to arrive at abstruse theological learning, but we want something which shall more directly prepare men, who have gone through a general education, for the practical duties of a clergyman.'[3]

There is a good deal of evidence that Wilberforce was right to be dissatisfied with traditional patterns of training. As early as 1835, over three hundred noblemen, MPs and clergy had petitioned the bishops on the unsatisfactory nature of pre-ordination training at the universities as 'too general and vague to have any sufficient bearing on the future usefulness of the Christian minister'. A couple of examples may put flesh and blood on the bones of that statement. R. W. Dixon, the future church historian, went up to Pembroke College, Oxford, in 1852, with a view to ordination, and later recorded: 'I did not find it in a good state. The Master did nothing in tuition except a Sunday lecture in Greek Testament. There was very little discipline, no social intercourse between the fellows and the undergraduates, and Collections were merely a nominal ceremony.'[4] William Morris wrote to his mother from Exeter College in 1855 to explain that he had decided to be an architect instead of a clergyman. He begged her not to think that 'you have as it were thrown away money on my kind of apprenticeship for the Ministry; let your mind be easy on this score; for ... an University education fits a man about as much for being a ship-captain as a pastor of souls.'[5]

Moreover, the universities were becoming, it seemed, steadily less clerical, less Anglican, and, some added, less Christian. From 1854, Dissenters were free to take degrees at Oxford. The 325 ordained Fellows of Colleges (out of a total 470) in 1845 had declined to 61 fifty years later.[6] The increasingly secular tone of Oxford moved John Keble to write gloomily to Sir J. T. Coleridge (11 December 1855): 'What sad accounts I hear of the Germanization and secularization of Oxford. I should think it would be very soon necessary for people who wish their sons to have a fair chance for being Christians to send them to some other place; and for Bishops to resort ordinarily to the Theological Colleges. ...'[7] Six months later, his pessimism was, if anything, deepened: 'Oxford I fear is too far gone (in the Germanizing way)—unless Cuddesden [*sic*] prove able to stop the decay: certainly there seems a great blessing on that place.'[8]

If Oxford was proving increasingly inadequate for theological training, why should Churchmen object to a college like Cuddesdon as an attempt to make up what was lacking? They objected partly because the very idea of separated seminaries for the education of the clergy seemed to smack of the Roman system. (Protestants tended to sniff Popery everywhere after Newman's departure for Rome in 1845 and the papal creation of English territorial bishoprics in 1850.) In 1852–3, when the Bishop of Lichfield tried to set up a diocesan seminary, there had been riots in Staffordshire. Segregated education of the clergy not only seemed Romish; it cut at a cherished principle of the Anglican Establishment, whose protagonists 'delighted to point out how men who were in various ways to take the lead in church and state underwent the same kind of education, picked up a common code of manners, accepted the same political allegiance and imperial responsibility'.[9] In 1860, H. N. Oxenham, an Anglican convert to Rome, commended the Anglican pattern to his fellow Roman Catholics: 'The mixture of those who are training for the Church with those who are preparing for the army, or the bar, or the medical profession, or the service of the state, is, I suppose, the main secret of the great moral and social influence of the Anglican clergy.'[10] To many Protestant minds, theological seminaries meant, if not Romanism, at least the encouragement of a separated clerical caste and an un-healthy and un-English sacerdotalism.

Another item on the charge-sheet against Cuddesdon was that it very rapidly developed into a party college, of a pronounced High Church—its enemies said 'Romish'—flavour. Samuel Wilberforce foresaw the danger, when he appointed Liddon, an ardent disciple of Dr Pusey, that the college might become, 'a mere collection of young men under Dr Pusey's direction'.[11] Liddon for his part abominated what he called 'the menagerie theory' of a theological college, which embraced men of a wide range of religious belief and practice within a single community —rather as the Church of England itself professed to do. A university had to tolerate such pluralism; a theological seminary need not. Moreover party spirit was liable to run higher at Cuddesdon, which, unlike the earlier diocesan colleges at Wells and Chichester, was residential, and so capable of a much more intense form of common life. Bishop Wilberforce was a moderate High Churchman, not an ultra like Liddon, and certainly no Romanizer. He wrote to Golightly on 23 September 1857: 'You are quite right in saying that I quite abhor Romish doctrine, but you are mistaken in thinking that I like Romish rites and ceremonies. Everything Romish stinks in my nostrils.'[12] He wrote feelingly, for by 1857 his brothers Henry and Robert, and his brother-in-law, the future Cardinal Manning, had all gone over to the Roman obedience. That very fact, however, in keen Protestant eyes, branded Samuel with a strong presump-tion of guilt by association, a guilt which inevitably rubbed off on Cuddesdon.

Yet the virulent opposition to Cuddesdon was not simply part of a general attack on Bishop Wilberforce. It centred also on Liddon, the young and brilliant Vice-Principal. Liddon promised the Bishop, before being appointed, that he would moderate his public teaching, and in particular would not recommend private confession *indiscriminately* to the students. Notwithstanding, he managed to give a very advanced High Church tone to the teaching, devotion and worship of the college. In dealing with a student like Frederick George Lee— one of the first entrants to Cuddesdon in 1854, and a man already strongly drawn to Rome—Liddon's influence had the effect of putting out a fire with petrol.[13] In the Michaelmas Term of 1858, two Cuddesdon students, J. A. Maude and Francis Burnand, joined the Roman Catholic Church. At this point Wilberforce pressed King to give him his full and frank opinion as to the state of the college. King wrote a twelve-page letter, with considerable personal diffidence, diagnosed 'something wrong' at Cuddesdon, and put his finger on Liddon as the cause of it: 'I think the cause of the wrong will be found in the dear Vice-Principal.'[14] By 1859, Wilberforce had had enough, and reluctantly required Liddon's resignation.

In Wilberforce's mind, King was to be the antidote to Liddon. The Bishop pressed him, without success, to take the Vice-Principalship. Liddon himself tried to draw King away from Cuddesdon to St Saviour's, Leeds, a great Tractarian centre, but King refused that too. He was sure he ought not to desert Cuddesdon in its hour of need, when morale was probably at its lowest in the history of the college. 'I do not think I ought to leave this place yet', he wrote, 'I hope by God's blessing I may do a little of that peculiar work here which is too insignificant to attract a stranger, but of which you know the value.'[15] At the same time, King was clear that Liddon's rigorism, his attempt 'to fit the Cuddesdon shoe on every foot', would not do. Mass production of a High Church clerical stereotype was both educationally and spiritually disastrous. Unfortunately, it had already begun to happen, as a revealing letter of the Bishop, written in this period, all too clearly shows: 'Our men are too *peculiar*—some, at least, of our best men. I shall never consider that we have succeeded until a Cuddesdon man can be known from a non-Cuddesdon man only by his loving more, working more, and praying more. I consider it a heavy affliction that they should wear neckcloths of peculiar

37

construction, coats of peculiar cut, whiskers of peculiar dimen-
sions—that they should walk with a peculiar step, carry their
heads at a peculiar angle to the body, and read in a peculiar
tone. I consider all this as a heavy affliction. First because it
implies to me a want of vigour, virility and self-expressing
vitality of the religious life in the young men. It shows that
they come out too much cut out by a machine and not enough
indued with living influences. Secondly, because it greatly limits
their usefulness and ours by the natural prejudice which it
excites. . . .'[17]

Wilberforce saw the college taking on a more and more exotic,
un-Anglican image, what with the men's 'tendency to crowd the
walls with pictures of the Mater Dolorosa, &c., their chimney-
pieces with crosses, their studies with saints'; and their eccentric
devotional practices were of a piece with these extravagant
visual aids. Visitors, noting 'the habit of some of our men of
kneeling in a sort of rapt prayer on the steps of the communion-
table, when they cannot be *alone* there', registered 'the feeling
of the strict resemblance to what they see in Belgium, &c., and
never in Church of England churches'.

The enemies of Cuddesdon could hardly have asked for a more
detailed corroboration of their worst fears. The cloistered hot-
house of the seminary had produced an exotic and unhealthy
growth, to sober Anglican eyes as out of place as an orchid in a
cottage garden. The want of 'vigour . . . virility . . . vitality' was
tantamount to admitting that some of the students, obsessed
with matters of gesture, vesture and posture, had become more
than a little effeminate. Did Wilberforce fear homosexuality? It
was no unreal possibility in the kind of close, pious huddle
Cuddesdon had become. It looked as though the whole pioneer-
ing venture in theological training was about to run into the
sand.

CHAPTER FOUR

Principal King

> Men were afraid of 'narrowing' tendencies. Theological colleges were called 'hot-houses', and bishops looked askance at them.
>
> Now what King did more than any one man was, in a very large measure at all events, to show that these prejudices were not really justified.
>
> *Owen Chadwick[1]*

AT the beginning of 1859, Cuddesdon faced a crisis. The first principal, Alfred Pott, had resigned, his health seriously undermined by the controversies raging about the college. Bishop Wilberforce had at last dismissed Liddon, the vice-principal. King, as chaplain, was the sole remaining member of the staff. Student numbers had fallen drastically to a mere handful of men. The college was viewed with grave suspicion in the diocese, despite the largely favourable report of the three archdeacons whom Wilberforce had commissioned to investigate Golightly's charges in 1858. The future looked bleak indeed.

The re-staffing of the college obviously involved crucial decisions. Good men were wanted, who would work together as a team—no more one-man bands of Liddon's kind—and who would, at the very least, restore a measure of stability and moderation to the place. On 4 December 1858, Wilberforce had offered J. W. Burgon of Oriel the principalship, though at that stage he had added a rider that Liddon must stay on as vice-principal. Burgon, a shrewd character, went to the heart of the matter in refusing the post: 'I have convinced myself that it would be about as reasonable to expect that a chronometer could keep time while half the mechanism is defective, as that the institution should work well while Liddon is there.'[2] By January 1859, Wilberforce had removed the spanner from the works by compelling Liddon to resign, and the way was open for a new beginning.

It may be said that the Bishop's appointment of Liddon was his one serious misjudgement in choosing the early members of the Cuddesdon staff. He did not repeat the mistake, and in the principal and vice-principal he chose in 1859 his normally impeccable instinct for the right man for the job re-asserted itself. He chose as his principal Henry Swinny, sometime Fellow of Magdalene College, Cambridge, and a man of transparent goodness. He was notably moderate in theology, a stance which commended him as strongly to Wilberforce as it made him un-acceptable to Liddon, who commented: 'Moderate opinions are not a fair and tolerable representation of the Revelation of God.'[3] King, who was always diffident about the adequacy of his own gifts, refused the vice-principalship, which went to W. H. Davey, a solid, sensible man, a good teacher, central in his church-manship, and co-operative in disposition. King as chaplain provided the only thread of continuity between the old regime and the new.

The new staff may have lacked Liddon's force and rigour in theology and devotion. They certainly lacked his extreme brand of churchmanship. What they did bring, however, was a common concern for the life of the college, an ability to work together, not as a group of individualists, but as a band of brothers. They also brought a more relaxed, human, balanced ethos into the place, without in any way abating the zeal Liddon had shown to produce ministers who would be lovers of God and men. Cuddesdon remained bracing, without being intense. Sport was brought quite naturally into the life of the college—riding, cricket, croquet. The windows of the hot-house were thrown open, and some welcome fresh air began to blow through. Insensibly, the tone of the college began to change. Quietly, steadily, in the old Tractarian manner, the three men cultivated their garden; and it began to bear fruit. When Swinny spoke at the College Festival of 1861, he characteristically 'attributed much to the common life of the students—the constant, loving, scarcely-felt control of men of kindred spirits, an influence which could not be found elsewhere'.[4] No doubt; but anyone who has lived in a small residential college will know that in the end the ethos of the place is one and indivisible, and that you cannot have a good spirit among the students if the staff are not devoted to the work, the men, and one another.

On Swinny's death in 1863, King, after five years as chaplain, succeeded as principal. Even before he became principal, he had played a considerable part in raising the morale of Cuddesdon from the trough into which it had fallen in 1859. In August 1862, Swinny had written to King, who was away from college, that Lear, a student who had severed an artery in an accident, was making a good recovery : 'He is going on famously, and his being laid by is drawing out all the best feelings of the men, who are, as he himself bears witness, like so many brothers. Thanks mainly to God's grace; mediately, to your example of self-negation.'[5] The strong influence King had exerted on the men was greatly multiplied after he became principal. His appointment was greeted with confidence and joy by students, colleagues, and the Bishop. Samuel Wilberforce praised Swinny's 'nobleness of spirit . . . true and tender sympathy . . . rare singleness of purpose . . . increasing saintliness', and added his conviction that King was 'one like-minded with him who has entered on his rest : one who had worked with him in life; and who, taking up the fallen mantle of the former prophet, set at once, and in the same strength, to continue and complete his work'.[6]

It encouraged King that Davey, as vice-principal, accepted so generously his appointment to the post for which Davey had been next in line of succession. Davey wrote in retrospect : '. . . the new Principal (so long known far and near as its beloved chaplain), whose appointment had been hailed by all with so much real enthusiasm and thankfulness, succeeded to the government of a College, now established in the past and made ready to his hand for the future, to be directed by him with a power and success of which his past work had been a happy anticipation and augury.'[7] The principalship, though he fitted it like a hand to a glove, made heavy demands on King. He had to be teacher, pastor, and—since the college had no bursar—

administrator and general factotum. As if all that were not
enough, he also became vicar of the parish of Cuddesdon, since
the cure went with the principalship. This dual role of principal
and parish priest suited him to perfection, but it was no light
burden. It was something, certainly, to put into the scale against
the weight of criticism that a theological college trained men in
a rarified and unnatural atmosphere, instead of in the parish
and on the job.

The Cuddesdon men were trained by a man who was actually
working a parish—visiting the sick, burying the dead, catechiz-
ing the children, taking the normal round of parochial duties
and services. It was that rare kind of pastoral training which is
analogous to medical students being trained in a teaching hospital.
The only parallel that springs readily to mind today is the great
Orthodox seminary of St Vladimir's, New York, where Father
John Meyendorff and his colleagues not only staff the seminary,
but work the parish; and where the college chapel serves also as
the parish church. King's students worshipped regularly in the
parish church as well as the college chapel, and it may well be
that this arrangement, then and later, acted as a brake on
liturgical extremism in the college. At all events, as late as 1904,
the ceremonial of the college eucharist was simple, exactly the
same in college chapel as in parish church. 'The eastward position is taken. The two Eucharistic lights are burnt at early
celebrations. Vestments are not worn.'[8]

King's letters during his principate, which lasted from 1863
to 1873 and set a decisive seal on the life of the college, are
mostly dated from 'Cuddesdon Vicarage, Wheatley'. He writes
to his colleagues and old students letters of spiritual direction
and pastoral advice, out of his own parochial situation. His letters
are filled with the needs of his parish and the care of his people.
He writes to a priest of 22 July 1871 : 'I am very glad your
school is doing well, and I am glad to see you have taken the
children to see the beasts. These little kindnesses do a great deal
of good. Our school is not what I could wish it to be. This year
the village was quite upset by scarlet fever, and the schools
closed, so it is not fair to judge, but still it is not up to the mark.

I hope, however, it will improve, for the master, I think, likes us, and is anxious to please. He is good at the organ, and, with the help of Mr. Eichbaum, the choir is very much improved. The services are quite pleasant now. We have had for nearly twelve months a children's service, at three, every Sunday afternoon. We sing a musical Litany and then catechise them. We are doing the Acts of the Apostles, and this and a few hymns and prayers takes about fifty minutes. The children are in the best part of the church, and we have the regular choir, so it is their own service, but several parents come and seem to like it. I like it myself very much. I enjoy talking to children. If you think you could have one I will send you one of our little Litany books.'[9]

It is a charming picture, and the college principal who had Sunday by Sunday to take the boys and girls through the Acts of the Apostles, was not likely, in lecturing his own men on the Fathers and Hooker during the week, to forget the object of the whole exercise: the faithful and effective cure of souls.

King's nephew and domestic chaplain at Lincoln, Fred Wilgress, in an intimate memoir written just after his uncle's death, was to recall his faithfulness as a parish priest: 'In spite of the great claims of the College, he never allowed the parish to suffer. He was continually looking after the spiritual welfare of his flock. He was at the beck and call of anyone in sickness or in trouble. During an outbreak of smallpox he diligently visited, and when no one dared to put the dead into their coffins he did it himself. . . .'[10]

In his role as theological teacher, King read hard to equip himself. At Oxford his health had limited him to a pass degree—he was advised not to read for honours—and he was always conscious of his need to deepen his reading. The wells from which he drew his most characteristic teaching were—apart from the Scriptures—the works of Plato, Aristotle (especially the *Ethics*), Dante (whom he read in Italian), Hooker, and Bishop Butler. James Swallow, one of his students who later became chaplain of Cuddesdon (1874–76), remembered his lectures on Christian Doctrine as 'a veritable *théologie affective*, in which the dry bones of dogma were clothed with the sensitive flesh of

living, loving devotion, and lit up with the glow of poetic con-
templation, often under the guidance of Dante'.[11] No doubt the
weekly devotional addresses or meditations which the principal
gave in chapel were of the same quality, as well as being a foretaste of the informal talks he was to give when he went to Oxford
as Pastoral Professor. His teaching married heart and head,
devotion and dogma, in a quite inimitable way. It comes as a
shock to some lay people to discover how easily life in a
theological college may breed irreverence in its members. As
medical students may toss human limbs and organs around in
the dissecting room or path. lab., so theological students may
handle with the same kind of flippancy the great doctrines that
constitute the corpus of the Faith—sin, redemption, grace and
glory. King's whole approach was a preservative against that
kind of occupational disease. He knew, with his friend Father
Benson of Cowley and all the great Eastern theologians, that
Christian doctrine is not only to be believed and thought, but to
be lived and prayed.

As a spiritual guide, King used the utmost tact and discrimina-
tion. No one could have been more sensitive or sympathetic to
the individual's peculiar needs. Yet his glance, though kind, was
searching. He was a realist who could prick the bubble of com-
placency or self-deceit with the surest touch. For James Swallow,
'intelligent sympathy' was the keynote of King's approach. He
and his fellow-students found themselves, 'most tenderly, yet
most unflinchingly, compelled to face our lives before God'.[12]
Another old student recalled : 'His dealings with individuals . . .
were full of sympathy, and were never allowed to interfere with
a man's own personal convictions. Sympathetic teaching was left
to do its own work according to the conscience of the individual.
Many a rebuke, a piece of unwelcome advice, was given in a way
that could give no pain to a sensitive nature. To one student on
Good Friday, who had eaten very little during the days of Holy
Week, he gave the following advice, "Dearest man, eat breakfast
and come down to the level of Yours, E.K." '[13] The contrast with
Liddon, who, in Bishop Wilberforce's words, '*must* reimpress
his exact self'[14] on his students, could hardly have been greater.

In the matter of private confession, which Liddon had deliberately fostered in the college, King again took a different line. Auricular confession was not only rare in mid-nineteenth-century Anglicanism, it was also a theological hot potato. To many informed churchmen, as well as to popular Protestantism, it reeked of Rome and sacerdotalism. When King became principal, one of the students asked him to hear his confession, and received the reply, 'Wait a little, I must make my own first.' It was not long before he rode into Oxford and made his confession to Dr Pusey at Christ Church. King himself was to become a notable confessor, especially after he was made Pastoral Professor in 1873, but he never pressed the confessional on any penitent.[15] In 1874, writing to a lady who had asked him to suggest a rule of life for her, he included a word on confession : 'I can only repeat the Church's advice, try and get on without it; if you can't, use it.'[16]

Perhaps this is the most appropriate point to take up the inference that some are bound to draw from Bishop Wilberforce's critique of the college,[17] that there was the danger, if not the actuality, of an unhealthy homosexuality at Cuddesdon. The lack of 'vigour . . . virility . . . vitality' in some of the young men suggests at least the possibility. Lord Elton, in his short study of *Edward King and Our Times*, even canvasses the suggestion that the modern critic, to whom 'the very idea of sainthood, of heroic virtue deriving from religious faith, is an affront', may want to press the charge 'that King's aura of radiant love was homosexual in origin. Until he went to Lincoln, it may be said, was not his work almost exclusively among young men?'[18] It was indeed. Moreover, he never married and showed no inclination to the married life, though his letters and sermons reveal a tender understanding of it in others. He was utterly devoted to his mother, though not abnormally so. To a sex-obsessed generation like the present one, his very celibacy may appear to constitute a *prima facie* case for regarding him as homosexual. The homosexuality question is said to have been broached soon after his death, and to have influenced the form of the great bronze statue which is his memorial in Lincoln cathedral. Oral tradition has it that the original intention was to have King confirming a young boy, since confirming the young was a part of his work he loved best. There was apparently some misgiving about the presence of the boy, and in the event the statue portrayed King, in his vestments and with his hand raised in blessing, but, sadly, with no child to bless.

Some kind of case can no doubt be put together in this way; but there is actually not a shred of evidence to sustain it. It rests on inference and supposition and hearsay; not, so far as I can determine, on fact. There is much to be said on the other side, too. If we look at the lives of some of the best-known Victorian homosexuals—A. E. Housman, Lytton Strachey, Edward Carpenter—one of the clearest facts about them is their sense of loneliness, anguish, and deep inner unhappiness. Now if there is one thing plain about Edward King it is that he was a truly happy man. Geoffrey Faber, in the chapter of his *Oxford Apostles* (1933) entitled 'Secret Forces', has a section called 'Virginity and Friendship'. In it he suggests that there was a high degree of homosexual attraction among men of the Oxford Movement like Newman and Hurrell Froude. He may well be right. Yet we have to be careful not to get our historical and cultural wires crossed here. Terms of endearment between men, and what seems to us highly emotional language, were much more common among upper and middle class Englishmen in the nineteenth century than they are today.[19] It may be as easy for us to misinterpret some of the Victorian evidence as it is for an English visitor to Nairobi to put two and two together and make five when he sees two young African men walking down the main street hand in hand. Far from being a sign of endemic homosexuality, it is merely a normal, completely accepted gesture of friendship and respect.

Moreover, those who knew King well could say of him that, for all his warmth of pastoral affection, 'you felt that he had himself well in hand, that he had disciplined that strong affectionate heart and that burning zeal, and this discipline showed itself in self-restraint and gentleness'.[20] The same was said of one of his closest disciples, in whom men recognized so much of

King's spirit, Berkeley William Randolph. Randolph was a student of King at Oxford, served as his domestic chaplain at Lincoln, and did the same kind of creative work as principal of Ely theological college as King did at Cuddesdon. Of Randolph his biographer can say: 'Above all he had a deep and disciplined affection for young men, and especially for the young men with whom he had to do at the Theological College. . . . This power of disciplined affection was one of his highest qualifications for his work.'[21]

There is more detailed and personal evidence still, from King's own lips. His contemporaries are agreed that he was a shrewd judge of human nature, a realist, knowing what was in man. It so happens that a digest of the lectures he gave on Pastoral Theology in the Oxford of 1874, has survived, being published in 1932 from the notebook of one of his students, Canon Frewer of Brede in Sussex. In dealing with some of the seven deadly sins, and the ways in which these may attack a clergyman, he has the following to say under the heading of 'Lust':

'*Affectiunculae* (little acts of affection). Beware of this. Often the preludes of sin. Love we must, but so as to be in heaven together.
Crebra munuscula (repeated little gifts). Petting. Weak acts of kindness.
The greatest bar to friendship is any kind of sinful love. (Memory of school days sometimes darkened by this: friendships just not right.) For lust is the very essence of selfishness.'

King goes on to warn his men of the need for eternal vigilance here: 'Let him that thinketh he standeth take heed.' He urges the need for moral purity and self-control, 'for the sake of freedom' and one's own peace of mind; because they will have to offer spiritual guidance to others; and supremely, 'Because we must follow Christ. At least let us be pure for the sake of others. He could be in public places and elsewhere. Alone with women of infamous character because holy, guileless, undefiled, separate . . . "For their sakes I sanctify myself." We want priests

47

who can go without scandal into Sodom, and draw men out. . . .'[22]

Lord Elton gives numerous other examples, though he may have misunderstood King's words, 'Some of us look back tonight to old school friendships when Satan was transformed into an angel of light'. Elton suggests that King here is referring to a process by which 'all the velleities of fleshly desire are not so much repressed as transmuted by the miracle of grace, so that the *eros* and the *epithumia* of the unregenerate, natural man are assumed into the *agapè* of the saint, become part of it and minister to its power, much as the base substance of coal is transmuted into the beauty and heat of flame'.[23] No doubt that could and did happen with King, but this passage hardly supports the point that Elton is wanting to make. The context, the parallel reference to school friendships being just not right, and the scriptural allusion to Satan transforming himself into an angel of light (2 Corinthians 11 : 14)—surely all these point to the meaning of this passage as a warning against lust. The danger is that what begins as innocent camaraderie among boys or young men may end in illicit homosexual relations. King saw the danger and clearly admonished his ordinands against it. He would surely not have been the man to condone or overlook any such distortion of the fellowship at Cuddesdon.

The life of the Christian community on the hill at Cuddesdon was, from many accounts, no common thing. Canon Scott Holland of St Paul's, who could never be a student there but was a frequent visitor, was so devoted to the place that he chose to be buried in Cuddesdon churchyard. On 2 June 1885, looking forward to the annual College Festival which he could not attend, he wrote to Mrs Mary Drew: 'I am thinking so of happy Cuddesdon, and of my immense self-denial in being here! [i.e. in London]. How blessed it will be! I do hope you will love it with a real Cuddesdon love, which stands quite alone among loves.'[24] Robert Milman, the later Bishop of Calcutta. a man brusque in manner and no sentimentalist, was a visiting lecturer at Cuddesdon during his early ministry. He was not given to overstatement, but is on record as saying, 'It was like a breath from the Garden of Eden before the door was shut'.[25] King's own description of the place was, 'a Christian higgledy-piggledy' —in other words, a true community of staff and men, with a minimum of rules, an overriding of social and intellectual barriers, no 'donship' or stiff Oxford formality, the whole life of the place directed towards 'absolute *oneness*, all higgledy piggledy'.[26]

Scott Holland's sensitive antennae gauged the quality of the shared life, even though he knew it only as a visitor and friend of the college : 'I suppose that Cuddesdon men will always say that, whatever else came out at Christ Church and Lincoln, still there was never anything quite so full of thrill as the old days on the blessed Hill, when King was Principal. The whole place was alive with him. His look, his voice, his gaiety, his beauty, his charm, his holiness, filled it and possessed it. There was an air about it, a tone in it, a quality, a delicacy, a depth, which were his creation. He could draw love out of a stone : and there was not a man of any type or character that did not yield to his sway. Great burly chaps, arriving alarmed and un-shaped, keeping their portmanteaux packed ready for a bolt, were at his feet before they knew where they were. There was nothing of the forcing-house, of the seminarist pose, as was popularly supposed. All was human, natural, free. "Here is one of my hot-house plants," I remember him saying at one of the annual luncheons, as he laid his hand on the enormous shoulders of a man who had stroked the Oxford boat to victory for four years running on the Putney course. It is hopeless to try to tell the wonder of those old days. All over England there are men who look back to them, as to a heavenly vision—to which, by the infinite mercy of God, they have not been wholly disobedient.'[27]

They were men like Canon Nathaniel Keymer, who died at Nottingham in 1923, having spent over thirty years of his long ministry as Rector of Headon, a tiny country parish in Notting-hamshire, which he held in his praying hands and served with love. 'Keymer is still remembered in the little village of two hundred souls where he lived for over thirty years. He was a faithful pastor, a regular visitor, a kind friend to all in trouble, and above all a most careful teacher. He published several books, based on the instructions he gave in catechism class, and his fame spread throughout the land. . . .'²⁸ He had spent one year at Cuddesdon under King, whom he revered to the end of his days. It was no passing 'thrill'—to use Scott Holland's word—that Keymer experienced at Cuddesdon, but a vision and a power which bore him on to the end. He never really retired—as King counselled a priest should not—but died in harness in his late seventies.

In 1873, after fifteen happy years at Cuddesdon, King accepted Mr Gladstone's nomination and became Regius Professor of Pastoral Theology at Oxford. He thought himself ill-equipped academically to take the post, but if ever a man knew the subject he professed, it was he. Despite the many raised eyebrows among the dons—for King had little of the technical apparatus of scholarship—in the event he took Oxford by storm, and had as far-reaching an influence at Christ Church as at Cuddesdon. He told his Cuddesdon students quietly in the chapel one evening after Compline that he must leave them for the Pastoral Chair. After the stunned silence of unbelief, men cried like children, even the hearty athletes among them whose names were household words in the university. What the wrench meant for King himself we can only surmise, but he lifted the veil a little in a speech he made twelve years later. In 1885, on the afternoon of 25 April, when he had just been consecrated Bishop of Lincoln, he spoke informally to the old Cuddesdon men who had presented him with communion vessels and other gifts for his private chapel at Lincoln. He spoke of the 'tremendous wrench' it had been to leave Cuddesdon, and tried to recapture the essence of the life there. 'At Cuddesdon, you know, we never thought of being Bishops. We didn't care for position or rank. Two things we did care for—the possession of the full counsel of God, and liberty to teach it in every way. We wished to offer up our life and be happy, blessed in ourselves, and with the privilege of giving that blessedness to others. This was what made Cuddesdon to be Cuddesdon, and drew us nearer to God and to one another, giving us the peculiar freedom and elasticity which made us so loose and free (though not wild) in head and heart. For our heads rested, bowed down before the full Catholic Faith, and our hearts were surrendered to be disentangled and disciplined, to find their rest when given up to God ("for our heart is restless, till it find its rest in Thee!"). We were brought to love God, and one another in God, in a real and special way, not understood by people unless they themselves knew what it was to be thus free. . . .'[29]

Blessedness, happiness, freedom, elasticity, surrender, discipline —these were the connotations of Cuddesdon for King and, it would seem, for many who shared the life with him. The one thing needful, the love of God and man, had been eminently real at Cuddesdon. Nearly thirty years after he had left the college, King shared with a later generation of men, at the college Festival of 1900, something of the peculiar glory of the place : 'There is something I feel about Cuddesdon which I cannot quite feel of any other place. It was here that I learned to realise more than ever I did before the possibility of the reality of the love of God and the love of man. Somehow at Cuddesdon the cloud of conventionality which hangs over us so constantly seemed to be lifted off, and we saw something more into the hearts and minds of others. My life here gave me hope of a higher life for myself and a higher life for other people too.'[30] In a modern theological college, men may often have three years together. King's men normally had only one. Yet what a year! In Christian community, not length of days, but quality of life is what matters, and it seems tolerably clear that somewhere mixed up in King's 'Christian higgledy-piggledy' there was a foretaste of the Kingdom of God.

CHAPTER FIVE

The Pastoral Professor

> How strangely different are the times, in which you return among us, from those in which you left us. Now the fight is not for fundamentals even, but as to the existence of a Personal God, the living of the soul after death, or whether we have any souls at all, whether there is or can be any positive truth, except as to Physics, &c. . . .
>
> . . . But we have a grand battle; I, for whatever time remains to me; you, during, I hope, many years of vigour. It is an encouragement that the battle is so desperate. All or nothing : as when the Gospel first broke in upon heathen philosophies, and the fishermen had the victory.
>
> *E. B. Pusey*[1]

So Professor Pusey wrote, rather gloomily, from his rooms in Christ Church to J. B. Mozley, the newly appointed Regius Professor of Divinity at Oxford, on a February day in 1871. Pusey clearly foresaw a battle royal between the defenders of the Christian Faith in the University, and the protagonists of a new pagan materialism. Mozley, a theologian of high calibre, was not daunted by the bleak anti-religious wind then blowing through Oxford, though he took the measure of the challenge that faced him. He was well-equipped to occupy the chair of divinity at such a time : orthodox without being obscurantist; open to new currents of thought; able to help undergraduates wrestle with the task of theological reconstruction in the light of new knowledge and new thought.

Pusey's words, though characteristically full of foreboding, are a fair index of the intellectual challenge to Christianity which King also had to face, when he joined James Mozley as a Canon of Christ Church and a Regius Professor in 1873. Few challenged Mozley's theological and academic fitness for his chair, however; many doubted King's. At Oxford, as at Cuddesdon, King had to face considerable criticism and hostility. The undergraduates of Christ Church merely twitted him for his High Church beliefs by hanging a surplice from a lamp post outside his house in Tom Quad. Other university comment was more barbed and unpleasant. W. E. Jelf, for instance, writing as 'A High Churchman of the Old School', published a swingeing attack on the Anglo-Catholic party in the Church of England, which included severe strictures on King. Jelf did not mince words : 'It is impossible not to feel the greatest distrust of the newly-appointed Pastoral Professor at Oxford. A man of no university distinction, his only recommendation seems to have been the success he has had at Cuddesdon, mainly by his personal influence, in training priestlings under the auspices of two Bishops of Oxford. At the Leeds Congress he is reported in *The Times* of October 12, 1872, as exhorting his hearers not to shrink from the discipline which the Church offered them in Confession and Absolution. What will Pastoral Theology become in his hands?'[2]

King had no illusions about his intellectual attainments, and characteristically acknowledged himself as coming to his Oxford chair, 'socially unknown, academically nothing'.[3] With his modest pass degree, he was perfectly well aware that he could not hold a candle to Jelf's brilliant First in classics. He had written no scholarly works. On paper, he must have looked a very odd choice for the post. Many people no doubt thought that Gladstone's well-known High Church views had overridden his sound judgement. Yet to dismiss King as an intellectual lightweight would be to over-value paper qualifications and fly in the face of impressive evidence. When his appointment was mooted, the Queen, Mr Gladstone and other ministers received 'some most strong letters' against his suitability. Tait, the Archbishop of Canterbury—no less—wrote twice to dissuade Gladstone from what he saw as a dangerous High Church appointment. 'I shall be very sorry', he urged the Prime Minister, 'if the appointment you mention takes place, for I fear it will greatly shake public confidence in the theological school at Oxford.'[4] High Churchmanship—aggravated by his association with Cuddesdon—and low intellectual calibre were the twin sticks his opponents used to beat King. Tait, indeed, tied the sticks together and suggested in a later account that King's High Church theological views had little attraction for 'the more intelligent' of the Oxford undergraduates.[5] Perhaps for Tait, as a Broad Church liberal theologian and hammer of the Anglo-Catholics, this particular wish was father to the thought; but, given King's academic background, the charge was plausible enough to those who did not know him personally. It was not only liberals and evangelicals who were dismayed at the appointment; King was not even the choice of the High Church leadership at Oxford!

In the event, King went to Christ Church, to the professorship, and to the heart of Oxford's malaise and controversy in religion, lacking the confidence of many leading churchmen. He confessed to his old Cuddesdon men in 1885, when he had just exchanged his professorial chair for an episcopal one, that twelve years before he had been 'in a dreadful fright at having to face learned Oxford',[6] and knowing how rancid academic attitudes can sometimes be, who can blame him? In the Oxford of 1873, King knew that he would inevitably be involved in the clash of Catholic and Evangelical; High Church and Broad Church; believer, agnostic and sceptic. Little wonder that, when he told his Cuddesdon men the news of his university appointment, he should have added 'that last Sunday he had been preaching about the Crown of Thorns, and now he was called upon to wear it—that he was called to leave Cuddesdon and go to Oxford'.[7] The reference to the crown of thorns was no passing phrase or pious exit line. King chose his words carefully, and later disclosed to Bishop E. S. Talbot that when he first came to Oxford he took the crown of thorns as his special theme of meditation, because it symbolized 'the Saviour's sufferings of the head'.[8]

One strand in King's crown of thorns was undoubtedly the hard study and wide reading which his professorship imposed on him. He was not a natural academic, and while he found study congenial enough in itself, he did not welcome the heavy inroads it made into his time. He was never the pure researcher. For him study was always grist to the mill of his preaching, teaching, pastoral care and counselling. He gave himself so freely to individuals that he was driven to carve out extra time for study, often late at night, working away at it—as he later advised his Lincolnshire clergy to do—'by the lamp of sacrifice'.

There was no doubt that the Professor of Pastoral Theology was himself a pastor of rare quality. Cuddesdon and his curacy at Wheatley had already shown that. As a theologian, on the other hand, he saw his serious need for a much fuller technical equipment. In the Long Vacation of 1875 he went to Germany to learn the language which would open the door to some of the best theological thinking of the nineteenth century. He had a week in Leipzig, where he met most of the leading theological professors, including Delitzsch, Ludthart, and Tholuck. The rest of his time he spent at Dresden, living with a devout Lutheran family, who helped him in his efforts to acquire the language in the shortest possible time.

He was impressed by the industry and book-learning of the German theologians, but detected a flaw in their approach : 'I think in England we have a wider-reaching, and better-balanced, work than the Germans have; they have confined themselves almost to the cultivation of the intellect. I don't think it will hold the *whole* man; he needs cultivation of Heart, Feelings, Affections, etc., as well.'[9] This refusal to isolate the intellect, in either theological training or general education, gives a clue to King's own cast of thought. Dr F. E. Brightman, the outstanding liturgist, who studied under King, and Dr William Bright, the distinguished Professor of Ecclesiastical History who was King's colleague,[10] both thought him 'among the most intellectual persons' they had known. Brightman glossed this claim, which to the Archbishop Taits and Jelfs of this world must have seemed more than a mite paradoxical, by adding : '. . . only, as was perhaps the case with St Anselm, to whom he has been compared, his intelligence was so much a part of his character, so wholly himself, that it might easily escape notice in the simplicity and charm of his personality. He had a singularly alert mind, and was interested in everything; no one ever saw him bored, and he never touched a topic without displaying an original view, and he was really alive to the intellectual difficulties of his day. He knew and could talk French, German, and Italian; and in a mixed company he could talk in at least three languages at once—no mean accomplishment; while his English was admirable, and he read widely to the end.'[11]

King came back to Oxford for the Michaelmas Term of 1875 with more than a working knowledge of German under his belt. He also brought back with him a vivid impression of the triumphant material progress in Germany, flushed with pride after its crushing victory over the French in 1871. At the same time he noted with disquiet how the life of the people had been corroded by the acids of unbelief : 'It is very interesting seeing the wonderful upgrowth and power of the German nation; but the unbelief is very sad—only three per cent, they say, go to any sort of church in Berlin, and unbelief is quite open. They seem to have passed through the stages of Rationalism and Pantheism, and now they have almost ceased to care about the metaphysics which we have been following, and *worshipping* in them, and they are devoting themselves to physics. This means, I fear, for many, *materialism.* Ludthard says this plainly, meaning by materialism love of money or power or pleasure; this seems to be the leading danger now—that people will try to be respectable, but without God; to separate morality from religion, to devote themselves to civilization and culture, and forget God.'[12]

King had gone to Germany and learned the language, not of course to study creeping materialism, but to gain direct access to the best theological scholarship, especially in his own field of Pastoral Theology. We know that he later drew, for his Oxford lectures, on the great three-volume *Pastoral Theology* of Johann Michael Sailer, a leading Roman Catholic theologian of the early nineteenth century, whose writings had made him a power in Germany. It seems likely that it was on this 1875 study-tour of Germany that King met Dr Döllinger, the outstanding liberal Catholic theologian, who in turn introduced him to Sailer's works.[13] Sailer, a contemporary of Goethe, had died as long ago as 1832, but both Döllinger and King found his work extraordinarily apt to their own age. Sailer, hailed today by theologians like Hans Küng as a herald of the more biblical and dynamic view of the Church associated with the Second Vatican Council, was a thinker who took the unbelief of his age with profound seriousness. The forty-two volumes of his works were all an attempt to take up the challenge of that rationalism of the eighteenth-century Enlightenment which underlies the massive turning away from Christianity in modern Europe. For Sailer, there was an enormous task of pastoral and theological reconstruction to be undertaken. King, from his experience of irreligion in Germany and in Oxford, endorsed Sailer's view and found in his German counterpart a kindred spirit. The works of Sailer were soon on King's study shelves, in constant use, and laid under contribution for his Oxford lectures. He remained faithful to Sailer long after he left Oxford, and as Bishop of Lincoln kept a portrait of the German Jesuit on an easel in a corner of his study at the Old Palace.

Sailer was part of that wider stream of European Christianity on which King drew at Oxford and throughout his life. Critics of nineteenth-century Oxford's religion are apt to dismiss it as insular, parochial, small-minded. These are not labels that can be justly pinned on King. He read his Dante, the towering prophet of human character under divine judgement, as many other Victorians did; but he read him in the original Italian. He also read Bishop Dupanloup, the great educationist and reformer of the Diocese of Orléans, in French; and Dr Döllinger in German. On his annual holiday abroad, he would make a point of visiting the local Catholic bishop, whether he was in France, Italy, Germany or Switzerland, and discuss with him his work and problems. King was English to the core, and utterly devoted to the Anglican Church; but he was no ecclesiastical Mr Pecksniff, continually expatiating on the merits of the Church of England, with an occasional bow to such other churches as there may happen to be.

King's debt to Sailer has never been explored. One suspects that Sailer himself, though a fascinating author, has had few English readers. Alexander Dru, the veteran member of the Benedictine community of Downside Abbey, has the measure of Sailer's worth in his Faith & Fact Book, *The Church in the Nineteenth Century: Germany 1800–1918*. Another Benedictine scholar, the German Dom Augustin Pütz, is at the heart of Sailer research on the continent. During his studies at Cambridge in the late 1960s, Dom Augustin was delighted to discover in Edward King an Anglican friend and student of Sailer.[14] It was, appropriately enough, an Anglican monk of Mirfield, recently returned from Germany to the mother house of the Community of the Resurrection, who gave me an offprint of Dom Augustin's article entitled, 'Bishop Edward King, an Anglican Friend of Sailer'. That Mirfield, the community founded by King's friend and admirer, Charles Gore, should have pointed up the Sailer-King connexion in this way seems altogether apt.

How much King was influenced by Sailer is not easy to say without much fuller research. King's pastoral lectures and his *Counsels to Nurses*—addresses he gave as the patron of the Guild of St Barnabas—both suggest that it must have been considerable. King's work on Sailer, a major German theologian, is one further ground for querying the easy dismissal of him as an intellectual nonentity at Oxford. The fact of his influence in the university is attested by many people. How, and how far, he influenced the members of the university, it is less easy to say. In our quest for Edward King, however, these crucial questions cannot be left on one side, and we must now tackle them as best we can. 'It may be doubted whether any man save J. H. Newman has exercised so strong an influence on the religious life of the university. It was brought to bear not only or even mainly through sermons, lectures, and books, but through personal relations with men of all kinds and ages.'[15] Those words, written about Charles Gore's influence at Oxford from

1875 to 1893, suggest the power which a man may wield as teacher and pastor through the complex web of his personal relationships. King certainly did so, but, partly because he had none of Gore's productivity as an author, his influence may easily be overlooked. The number and quality of the Oxford men who came under King's spell are both impressive. The scholarly liturgist F. E. Brightman; the historian W. H. Hutton; G. W. E. Russell, author, parliamentarian and King's first biographer; Francis Paget, Dean of Christ Church and Bishop of Oxford; Winnington-Ingram, Bishop of London; B. W. Randolph, Principal of Ely Theological College; these are only a few of the men on whom King made a permanent mark.

Hutton, writing soon after King's death, looked back over thirty years to the course of pastoral theology lectures he had heard King give in the Oxford of 1880 : 'It is a memory which to hundreds of those who share it is one of the most precious things in their lives. We remember those crowded lectures, so fresh and unconventional yet so full of meaning and value, so lastingly impressive; I expect that for many like me he was the only professor all of whose courses were attended, and that for pure pleasure and profit.'[16] It so happens that a set of notes from King's pastoral theology course of 1874 has survived in the notebook of one of his students. The notes were published by Eric Graham, the then Principal of Cuddesdon, in 1932.[17] Though hastily written in student 'telegraphese', the notes are perfectly intelligible, and convey something of the quality of the pastoral professor—'so human, so sagacious, so penetrating, so devout,'[18] as Bishop Talbot described his teaching.

Why were the lectures so popular? They had certain obvious attractions. They were written in the best 'King's English', and his style was always lively, witty, salted with homely and proverbial expressions. He was never ponderous or hyper-academic in manner. His own gentle brand of humour kept breaking through continually, as when he advised his students, 'to consult, on some critical point of divinity, the works of So-and-so, "in thirty-two volumes", and, when the laugh had come, adding quietly, "folio" '. Or again, to illustrate the advantage to a clergyman of absence of pride, he told his class the pleasure it had given him to receive a letter beginning, 'Dear Sir,—I never mind writing to you, for when I write to you I never feel that I am writing to a gentleman.'[19] At other times, the humour had a sharper cutting edge to it, as when he dealt with some of the protean forms that pride may take—vanity, self-complacency, showing off . . .—and added a word on '*Castles in the air* : Smash them up, for your own arms are sure to be emblazoned over the castle door.'[20]

A pungent style, spiced with humour, no doubt got the lectures off to a good start. But there was far more to their appeal than that. King drew on an extraordinarily wide range of material for the lectures : from biblical sources, naturally, and especially from the portrait of Jesus in the Gospels as the Good Shepherd, the pastor *par excellence*. Take, for example, his use of the account of Christ's encounter with the Samaritan woman at the well of Sychar. He urges his ordinands to notice the 'patience and thoroughness in dealing with individual souls' which Jesus reveals here : 'He tired, hungry, and thirsty. (Don't grumble if called out at dinner-time or bed-time.) Patience with her roughness and ignorance. Leads her on to "call her husband", i.e. to her sin. Encourages—catches hold of the one thing praisable—"In that thou hast well said." '[21] He also drew, of course, on the Early Fathers and the Schoolmen : on St Bernard of Clairvaux, on St Gregory's classic treatment of *Pastoral Care*; on St Augustine and St Chrysostom; St Basil and St Bonaventura. He would also cite standard Roman Catholic divines like Massillon and Lacordaire. To the Bible and Book of Common Prayer, he added the normative Anglican authors : Hooker, Andrews, Jeremy Taylor, Bishop Bull. He freely quoted the great Tractarians, whose disciple he was : Newman, Pusey, Keble, Marriott, Liddon, Mason Neale. Yet at the same time he found fruitful matter for training in pastoral understanding in the works of Juvenal, Suetonius, and Aristotle. We find him, under 'self-examination', pointing his men to the questions which John Wesley devised for the members of his 'band-meetings' : '(1) What have I done wrong? (2) What great temptations have I escaped? (3) What have I said or done of which I am not sure whether it is sin or not?'[22]

The full range of the material he drew on was wider still. The scope and variety of the reading he recommended for moral theology tickled his undergraduates, for the books 'ranged from the Baptist Yearbook to the Ignatian Exercises, from the Catena of Chinese Buddhism to the best sporting novels'.[23] In the *Pastoral Lectures*, we find him urging his men: 'Read good novels. You will thus travel into circumstances and conditions, and situations of life.'[24] He regarded nothing human as foreign to himself, and so cast his net as widely as possible. When he came back to Oxford, he re-read Aristotle's *Ethics* as a way of strengthening his grip on basic humanity: 'To go from the Bible to Aristotle is to go *back* and to go *down*, and to narrow your hold on, and your sympathy with, men.'[25]

The lively presentation, the wealth of source material—these were important; but even more King's lectures drew men because they mediated his profound sympathy with all sorts and conditions of men. It is the same sympathy we find in his letters and sermons, and in all his pastoral dealings. The width of his sympathy determines the breadth of his reading, so that we can say of the *Pastoral Lectures*, with infinitely more truth than we can of the *News of the World*, that all human life is there. King would undoubtedly have agreed with Bishop Kenneth Kirk, who quotes his predecessor at the opening of his study of Moral Theology, that 'The aim of moral theology is ... to accumulate from every available source whatever information will be of use to the priest for his task of shepherding individual souls.'[26] King's breadth of mind is the more impressive because it belongs to a convinced High Churchman, strongly committed to the Tractarian position. He has the conviction, without the narrowness or the fussy, blinkered 'churchiness', which so often threatened to corrupt Tractarianism. Francis Paget, in a book dedication to 'The most reverend father in Christ, Edward bishop of Lincoln', saw him not only as an 'exemplar of obedience' but as 'a defender of liberty'.[27] King stunned his High Church friends, and roused the wrath of the Dean of Lichfield,

by publicly defending divorce where the pastoral facts of the
case warranted it. Randolph and Townroe, who both knew him
well, speak of him as 'a broad-minded man with a very shrewd
judgement. He would give very sound and good advice on many
subjects which might have no bearing at all on ecclesiastical
matters. He possessed a gift of sanctified commonsense and
worldly wisdom which was apt to surprise those who only knew
him at a distance.'[28] King was a good judge of character, who
could spot a rogue quicker than most and knew integrity when
he saw it. His deep-set blue eyes were kind, but piercing—very
uncomfortable to look into if you were trying to impose on him
or evade the truth. Ronald Knox used to say that when you
looked into King's eyes, you saw into another world; and no
doubt the heavenly-mindedness was there. It was combined,
however, as in so many of the saints of God, with a very keen
sense of the realities of this present world, in which he was by
no means an innocent abroad.

Francis Paget, as an undergraduate at Christ Church, heard
King preach in the cathedral in 1873, the year he took up his
professorial chair. Paget described him as 'an elderly canon'—
King was forty-three!—but was chiefly impressed by the quality
of his preaching and by his liberal, hopeful attitude. He wrote
to his sister after the service from his lodgings in St Aldate's:
'One is so ready to praise even moderately good sermons, that
one has no words left to extol such preaching as his according
to or nearly according to its deserts. He speaks without either
notes or hesitation ... I think that a liberal High Churchman is
the very best thing that the world, or even Oxford, can show; and
to see an elderly canon, perfect in every detail of culture, standing up to say such things as King said this morning, is a most
happy confirmation of one's faith in humanity, present and
future ...'[29] One could wish that Paget had given his sister some
details of the sermon's content, but the impact is clear; and
Paget, who succeeded King in the Pastoral Chair, was a dis-
criminating judge. Though we do not know what King said on
that occasion, we know that his own recipe for a good sermon

was 'Church doctrine, Catholic phraseology, Study of Scripture, and the whole tied together by love'.[30]

Paget is only one among many witnesses to the breadth of King's sympathy and the amplitude of his view; and the breadth and amplitude must not obscure the truth that King's teaching was utterly Christ-centred. He was willing to learn from anyone and from any experience, to cite Aristotle or Buddha or whoever else could help him understand the human condition and the ways of men. But his touchstone remained Jesus Christ. Not that his view of Christ was narrow. He had in fact a keen sense of the inexhaustible significance of the Word made flesh. He urged his students, his pastors in the making, to embrace the *Imitatio Christi*—'we have to be like Him, if we are to set a proper example'—and reminded them that though the life of Christ could never be completely written, it could be fully lived : 'You can't write a whole "life of Christ." None of the Fathers tried for a thousand years—until S. Bonaventura. They wrote commentaries on His words, miracles, etc. Christ lives in His saints. We know His life in them. S. Paul prayed to know the "*power*" of His Resurrection, though he knew the *fact*. Christ's life extends from eternity to eternity. Only a small portion contained in the fragmentary memoirs of the Gospels.'[31] All the crucial marks of the Christian pastor, he found in the life of Jesus— patience, courage, solitude, humility, prayer, and 'unchanging love' : 'He "loved" the young man; Mary and Martha; S. John. He asked for Peter's love, and "to the end." We let our love grow cold, e.g. to the boy who reaches a rugged manhood; who begins to have opinions of his own, and affections settled on others. No gentlemanly substitutes for love (e.g. patronage) will do.'[32]

King's influence on undergraduate Oxford was not confined to his lectures and sermons. His lectures lacked a formal setting, since he gave them 'in his own house, standing in the doorway between study and dining room, and dressed in a cassock'.[33] The homely surroundings and the pastoral garb are symptomatic of his whole approach. Equally homely and pastoral, and even freer of academic restraint, were the talks and meditations he gave in the disused wash-house at the bottom of his garden in Christ Church, which he called his 'Bethel'. He described how it all began in a letter written at the start of the Easter Term of 1876 : 'Term is just beginning. We get along very nicely, I am thankful to say. Last term I started a little "Bethel" in my garden; it was a wash-house, and we cleaned it out and put cocoa-nut matting and chairs and a Harmonium—very simple, but very lovely. We had a sort of Meditation every Friday evening at 8 p.m. We did the Seven Deadly Sins just like Cuddesdon. I enjoyed it immensely. We are having them again this Term, only at 9 o'clock, because of the boats! Poor things, they were so good; the place was crammed.'[34] The crush must have increased, since King started with a handful of undergraduates and ended with three hundred,[35] though they could hardly all have squeezed in at the same time, to judge from surviving photographs of the Bethel. Many of them were not ordinands, though some came to ordination through King's influence, like the young clergyman from Northamptonshire whom Scott Holland met in 1883 : 'I saw an "Angel" last night, a Mr——, from some living in Northamptonshire, beautiful, intelligent, thoughtful, charming . . . He knows men I think; rowed in his boat at Oxford; then got wholly snared by King.'[36]

It is an interesting touch in King's account that the time of the Bethel meetings was put back to nine o'clock in the summer term, 'because of the boats', in other words, to allow men to get back to college after rowing on the river. We glimpse the width of King's appeal here. The men who came to Bethel, it seems, were not a pietistic remnant, pale young curates in the making. They were a good cross-section of the young manhood of Oxford, and included plenty of rowing men. In fact the hearties as well as the aesthetes, the tough and the tender, the clever and the simple, all came to King. When he left Oxford for Lincoln, over three hundred B.A.s and undergraduates joined together to present him with his episcopal ring, in thanks for all the spiritual help he had given them, especially through his Bethel.[37] It is hardly likely that those three hundred men were all of a special 'religious' type. In fact King's humanity and goodness drew all kinds of men to him, including some of the most unlikely. Even the young A. E. Housman, already then no doubt incubating the melancholy he would later express in *The Shropshire Lad*, felt the fascination. As an undergraduate at St John's he heard King preach a University Sermon in 1878, and described his impressions in a letter to his father: 'On the Sunday before last, Canon King of Christ Church preached at St Mary's on 'binding and loosing'—a counterblast to Dean Stanley in the *Nineteenth Century*. The sermon was unconscionably long, and considerably over our heads, brimming as it did with patristic learning, until, at the end of an hour and a quarter, he concluded with an apology to his younger brethren for having bored them, and giving as his reason that Our Lord grieved Peter, which I did not quite see the force of. But I felt it was quite worth sitting still for an hour and a quarter to watch such an interesting personality. He is tall, but stoops; and haggard in the face but without grey hair; and his sermon was most masterly here and there. The exquisitely deprecating way and affected timidity with which he put forth his strongest points, and the mournful and apologetic modulation of his voice where he was pulling Dean Stanley to pieces, were really almost worthy of Disraeli, and not altogether unlike, were it not for the deadly earnest, which was rather detrimental to the oratorical effect.[38]

Young Mr Worldly Wiseman rather spoils the force of his own criticism that King's preaching was marred by affectation and a striving for oratorical effect, by acknowledging the 'deadly earnest' in which he spoke. No one else ever, to my knowledge, accused King of being theatrical in the pulpit. Many spoke of his direct and downright manner, which gave his words weight, and in which, like Cromwell, he 'spoke *things*'. The point to note is that this was a *university* sermon—hence its length and its patristic quotations. As for the supposed 'affected timidity', we can understand, what the young Housman could not, that when he preached to the senior members of the university, King felt genuinely timid and at an academic disadvantage. For all that, though never 'snared' by King, Housman was obviously drawn to him, be his religious opinions never so outrageous.

Brightman says of King, 'no one ever saw him bored'; rather, he was 'interested in everything', and we may add, in everybody. It might be a young fourteen-year old, up from Cornwall to sit his Oxford Certificate Examination, who chanced to meet Canon King in the Broad Walk at Christ Church. No matter; King would gladly walk and talk with the lad. The boy was in fact Arthur Quiller-Couch ('Q' to the multitude of his later readers), who was to become the celebrated author and a Professor of English Literature at Cambridge. Q recorded the incident ('that gracious episode') over half a century later, in his account of the spell Oxford cast over him during this first encounter : 'I shall say no more of those enchanted three or four days save to correct with fact a small incident in a story of mine, *The Ship of Stars.* Actually, I was standing at gaze in the empty Broad Walk of Christ Church, my imagination peopling it with the crowd described in *Tom Brown at Oxford* as parading there on Com- memoration Sunday, when two elderly clergymen emerged from the Meadow Gate, halted on some kindly instinct to question me, and made me share their walk by the river, the College Barges (naming each one for my eagerness), and so up beside the Cherwell. The real figures in that gracious episode were two Canons of Christ Church—Bright and Edward King, afterwards famous Bishop of Lincoln; the latter converted in my novel into the even more famous and perhaps equal in saintliness (he couldn't be saintlier) John Ruskin.'[39]

One would give a good deal to know how well Q, who went up to Trinity College in 1882, came to know King during his undergraduate years. (A description of Bethel from Q's pen would be a marvellous addition to the gallery of portraits we have of King.) His autobiography shows him wrestling with religious and philosophical issues in the early 1880s. Did he find any light from King's teaching?

Through his lectures, sermons, and Bethel addresses, King influenced the undergraduates. Yet some of his profoundest work was done in private, as confessor and spiritual director. Jelf, in lashing out against King's appointment in 1873, had shuddered at what he would do in Oxford through advocating 'the discipline which the Church offered . . . in Confession and Absolution'. King proved to be no fanatic about the confessional, though he treasured its rightful use in the Church of England. He himself would go to confession two or three times a year, and 'his feeling about this matter in later life was, that it would not be amiss if some of the people who use Confession very frequently would go less often; while he wished that many who never go to Confession would do so now and then'.[40]

As a confessor he combined strength with tenderness. His letters of spiritual counsel show how stern he could be when confronted by pride or stubborn folly. Yet the prevailing tone of his dealing with his penitents was one of gentleness and hope. 'No one was more tender and gentle with his penitents (and he heard many confessions), no one more sensitive to the sorrows of others. Yet he was a man of unconquerable hopefulness.'[41] He was a great encourager, and would often urge a man or woman, 'You must not let temptation take the heart out of you. You must go bravely and quietly on.'[42]

B. W. Randolph was one of many undergraduates who made their first confession to King. Dons came too, including men of the calibre of J. R. Illingworth, philosophical theologian and a key contributor to the liberal Catholic symposium, *Lux Mundi* (1889), who made King his regular confessor.[43]

In addition to his work as confessor, and his counselling of individuals, King was heavily involved in Oxford projects for Christian missions and education. He took the keenest interest in the universal mission of the Church, which, he confessed, 'always stirs me up to the very bottom'.[44] There is little doubt that, had his health been stronger, he would have gladly gone overseas himself. At the age of sixty, he could write to one of his young chaplains, 'I am off to China by the first boat! Will you come? I am just back from the meeting where a beautiful C.M.S. missionary straight from China has been preaching—at least what *I* call preaching—talking the Gospel with all the fervour of a living missionary. Most crushing! Eleven years and no results, and five deaths! Then three converts, and then another death! Then another year, and then 7,000! And such beauties! My dear child, if you and I get just in, it will be only by holding on to the extremist tip of one of their pigtails!'[45]

This zest was no fitful temper with King. He was a leading founder of St Stephen's House, Oxford, a missionary training college for priests. The Oxford Mission to Calcutta—a missionary brotherhood of Oxford men working among educated Indians —was first mooted at a gathering in King's rooms at Christ Church in 1879.[46] The inspiration for the mission sprang not only from a letter of Bishop Douglas on Indian missions, but also from 'the inspiring lectures of Dr King on work for Missions as a necessary part of parochial efficiency'.[47] Nearer home, and giving Mrs Jellaby the lie, King was a strong supporter both of the Christ Church Mission, Poplar,[48] and of the Oxford House settlement in Bethnal Green. He was a strong supporter of the two colleges—Keble and Lady Margaret Hall —set up on a definitely Anglican basis during his time at Oxford,[49] and preached at the opening of Keble College Hall and Library on 25 April 1878. He took as text, 'None of us liveth to himself' (Romans 14:7), and proceeded to draw out some of the universals of a university education: 'we truly educate when we educe, draw out, unfold, not the accidents of an individual, or of a class, or of a country, or of an age, but when we educe, draw out, unfold, perfect that common humanity which is in every man, wherever and whatever he may be.'[50] He spoke of service to the whole world, and of England's 'special obligations to India, and to Africa, and Australia'. He ended with a reference to Mrs Coombes' gift to Keble Chapel of Holman Hunt's painting of Christ as 'The Light of the World'. 'We have the hall and the library, but today we have yet another gift which is the key to all our treasures—a widow's mite, indeed, giving in its immediate and essential teaching more than all. There is but One Light that lighteth all the world, and we Christians have that Light. It is no mere human philosophy, no mere social progress to which we trust; but we trust in Him Who is the Light that lighteth every man that cometh into the world. It matters not in what age or what country. All things were made by Him, and in Him all things still consist; in Him we find our true relation to mankind; in His way, in His truth, and in His life, we may educate not ourselves only, but the world.'[51]

Professor King produced at Oxford no works of technical scholarship. Like that great French saint, the Abbé Huvelin, he preferred to 'write in souls'; to draw out, perfect, unfold, 'that common humanity which is in every man'; and to do it by the light of Christ.

CHAPTER SIX

Lincoln: 'A Bishop of the Poor'

> I have, as you know, no great gifts, but, by God's goodness, I have a great and real love of His poor; and, if it should please Him to let me be the bishop of His poor and enable me to help them to see more what they are to Him and what He is to them, I think I shall be happy.
>
> *Edward King, 1885*

WHEN King was appointed to the bishopric of Lincoln in 1885, it was clearly a wrench to leave Oxford after twelve happy years at Christ Church. Yet in some ways the move was congenial. His mother, to whom he was devoted, had died in 1883, and left what he called 'a terrible loss and blank'[1] in his home and heart. Neither Oxford nor life would ever be quite the same again without her. Again, Lincoln beckoned him, as a rural diocese, for King was country born and bred, and had often looked back longingly to his days as curate of Wheatley. Lincoln offered him a primarily pastoral role instead of an academic one, and he was above all else a pastor. In 1871, he had written from Cuddesdon : 'I have been obliged these last few years to spend the best of my time in reading, but if I should be free from the college I should go on in a parish just as we used to at Wheatley.' In Lincolnshire he would be able to fulfil again that vocation to the country poor which he had found at Wheatley : 'Our dear country poor,' his letter continued, '—for I feel more suited to them than others—require to be helped one by one. They are very ignorant, have very little time, work very hard, and often with poor food; they require a great deal of loving watchful sympathy. If it please God, I should rejoice to give myself wholly to spiritual work.'[2]

The same longing came out again six years later, when he wrote to a priest who had itching feet and was asking King to help him find a new appointment: 'May I venture to ask whether you have considered finally the necessity for change? . . . One often does most when one is not most aware of it. *I* should not choose the University to work in if I had my choice. I would rather be with the simplest agricultural poor, but it is not so arranged.'[3] Not many clergymen can have written in this strain from an Oxford chair and a Christ Church canonry, we may surmise; but there is no question that King meant every word he wrote, and his coming episcopate was to prove it. In 1885 it was 'so arranged', he had his desire, and his regret at leaving Christ Church was tempered by the thought of the pastoral work which opened out before him, in a setting free of the scepticism he deplored at Oxford.[4]

King came to Lincoln, as he had gone to Cuddesdon and Christ Church, with the hornets of controversy buzzing about his ears. There were many Anglicans—Queen Victoria among them—who could not easily stomach the idea of a strong High Churchman on the bench of bishops. Gladstone, as Prime Minister and prime mover of bishops on the ecclesiastical chess board, thought otherwise and was looking for a suitable candidate. A distinguished High Churchman and lay theologian himself, he was determined to give the Tractarians a place in the sun. Gladstone's thoughts turned first to Canon Henry Liddon, King's old colleague at Cuddesdon, whose superbly eloquent preaching was drawing great crowds to St Paul's. Liddon was obviously episcopal timber, from many points of view: a major theologian and apologist; of immense charm of manner; and one of the strong men of the Church of England. Yet though he was Gladstone's first choice, both the Queen and Archbishop Benson were set against him, as just the kind of rigid and inflexible High Church leader who would do most harm as a bishop.

Ironically, it was Archbishop Benson, who was later to sit in judgement on King when he was charged with ritual offences, who brought his name forward as an alternative High Church candidate for one of the three bishoprics—London, Exeter, Lincoln—recently fallen vacant. Though favouring him as a bishop, Benson did not think Lincoln quite right for King, who, he reported, 'is a very living power in Oxford. His kindling power would be a little lost on Wiltshire Downs or Lincolnshire Wolds.[5]

In the event, Liddon turned down the offer of Lincoln, and Gladstone wrote to King on 28 January 1885. In his letter the Prime Minister referred to Bishop Christopher Wordsworth's resignation on grounds of ill-health, and added: 'The expectations of the Diocese, after the Episcopate of Bishop Wordsworth, will be high, and I can make no better provision to save disappointment than by the proposal which I now submit to you.'[6] King accepted and, in all innocence, wrote to tell Liddon the news. Liddon, who had agonized over his own refusal, sent a generous note in reply: 'I am indeed delighted and thankful ... When I think of Oxford and all that your removal must mean —I cannot get on any further; only let me say that I am glad indeed, for the sake of the Church at large, that this consideration did *not* make you hesitate to accept.'[7] Charles Gore was another friend who found the news bitter-sweet: 'King is ideal for Lincoln, but oh! the blank it will be here. It is not to be thought of. Oxford will not be the same place at all. Ugh! it is grim.'[8]

Gladstone heard 'nothing but praises of the nomination to Lincoln', as he later told King. Bishop Wordsworth's response to the news was simply, *Deo Gratias!* Nor was it only High Church friends who wrote gratefully of King's appointment— Dean Church, Francis Paget, Butler of Wantage. For these men, his appointment was a notable Tractarian breakthrough into the leadership of the Church. Yet Bishop Stubbs, the great constitutional historian, and Dean Liddell of Christ Church ('Alice in Wonderland's' father and a theological liberal) wrote just as warmly. Liddell, as Dean of Christ Church, expressed the general wish of his undergraduates that King should preach once more in the cathedral—also the college chapel—before he left Oxford. He closed by adding, 'And I trust that, possibly at some future time, we may often hear a voice which has touched many hearts, and which none hear without wishing to hear it again.'[9]

Some of King's friends wrote like prophets new inspired as they looked forward to the shape of things to come in Lincoln-shire. Scott Holland poured out blessings on King's head, and assured him : 'It shall be a Bishopric of Love—The Love of God behind, and above, and about you! The Love of the Blessed Spirit, alive with good cheer within! The Love of the Poor shining out from you, until they kneel under its lovely benediction.'[10] In the same lyrical vein, Holland rhapsodized to his friend, Mary Drew (Gladstone's daughter), when she let him have the news—from the most impeccable source—of her father's nomination of the new Bishop of Lincoln : 'Bless you for the Surprise and Delight of King! A S. Francis de Sales at Lincoln! A joy like an old Spring, if you can fancy Spring grown old . . . He will move as a benediction.'[11] A little later, he wrote more soberly, 'King is, I hear, rather in misery at all that is before him, and will need a strong Dean.'[12] Here Scott Holland's pen seems to have run away with him in the opposite direction. King may well have been miserable at the thought of a mass of episcopal administration—always something of a hairshirt to him—but not, surely, at *all* that was before him? The countryside, the country people, the care of his clergy, his ministry to the poor : did these depress him? Surely not.

The letters of rejoicing and good wishes came not only from ecclesiastics and leading churchmen, but also—to King's delight —from the poor : from a prisoner in Wandsworth jail; from a worker at Carter's Nursery at the Crystal Palace; from a miner in 'the bowels of the earth'.[13] King wrote to his former student, E. S. L. Randolph, now a missionary in Zanzibar, '. . . now I am to go back to the cure of Souls, and be a shepherd again of the sheep and the lambs. This is my great delight, that He means it as a proof of His love, and that He means me to be a Bishop of His Poor! If I can keep that before me I shall be happy.'[14]

He was elected Bishop of Lincoln by the Dean and Chapter on 20 March 1885, and a month later his election was solemnly confirmed at Bow Church. A cloud no bigger than a man's hand apears in a light-hearted letter King wrote to a friend on 23 April, the day of the Confirmation : 'I have just been Confirmed. Nobody objected, in spite of the earnest appeals of the great Lawyers for some one to come forward. So, dear Friend, it shows that all these doctrines and ways which the good Ch. Ass. has been putting together, are within the limit of the Law (as well as the Creed!) for, if they thought they had a chance, no doubt the good people would have been kind enough to help me back to Oxford.'[15] The 'good Ch. Ass.' was the ultra-Protestant Church Association, and King had by no means heard the last of them. Bishop Magee of Peterborough dubbed them 'the Persecution Company Limited', and they certainly gave no quarter to High Churchmen who in their view broke the rubrics of the Book of Common Prayer. They could smell Romanism a mile away, and were bent on curbing 'ritualism'—a term they interpreted elastically—by using the full rigour of the law. They held their hand in 1885, though they were no doubt incensed and dismayed at King's appointment. Four years later they struck. The tiny cloud had by then become a storm-ridden sky which broke over King's bowed head and brought him untold misery. The letter of 23 April admirably illustrates Owen Chadwick's description of him at this time—'this happy, holy, serene, popular and harmless man'. His consecration was to bring him, in due course, into 'a world of unforeseen entanglements, which slowly gripped him, until for a time they almost destroyed his happiness'.[16]

King, always hopeful and willing to believe the best, went forward to his consecration at St Paul's on 25 April. A congregation of two thousand heard Canon Liddon preach a clarion call of a sermon, which must have put as much fire into the bones of Anglican High Churchmen as John Knox's did into the Scots armies. 1 Corinthians 4:15 ('For though ye have ten thousand instructors in Christ, yet have ye not many fathers . . .'), was his text, and he proceeded to extol King as 'a Father in Christ'. The sermon included what in Africa would be called a powerful 'praise-song' in honour of King. Yet where the 'praise-song' is apt to be fulsome, according to custom, Liddon's words were sober truth : 'Never, probably, in our time', he reminded his congregation, 'has the great grace of sympathy, controlled and directed by a clear sense of the nature and sacredness of revealed truth, achieved so much among so many young men as has been achieved, first at the Theological College of Cuddesdon, and then from the Pastoral Chair at Oxford, in the case of my dear and honoured friend. He is surrounded at this solemn moment by hundreds who know and feel that to his care and patience, to his skill and courage, to his faith and spiritual insight, they owe all that is most precious in life, and most certain to uphold them in the hour of death.' As Liddon's splendid periods rolled and echoed across the great spaces of the cathedral, they must have set up a strong resonance in the minds of many of his hearers. Did he carry them with him as he swept to his peroration, or did they feel that here his oratory over-reached itself? 'Certainly,' the preacher concluded, 'if past experience is any guarantee of what is to come, if there be such a thing as continuity of spiritual character and purpose, then we may hope to witness an episcopate, which ... will rank hereafter with those which in point of moral beauty stand highest on the roll of the later English Church—with Andrewes, with Ken, with Wilson, with Hamilton.'[17] Did even the preacher, one cannot help wondering, realize how utterly his words were to be fulfilled—in full measure, shaken together, pressed down, and running over?

King was overwhelmed by prayers and good wishes from all those, and they were many, who saw his appointment as completely right. Yet by no means everyone rejoiced. Many saw him as a menace to Evangelical Protestantism, and a portent of popish things to come. At his first entry into the Diocese of Lincoln, there was a predictable outcry against his alleged Romanizing tendencies. (In point of fact, like many High Churchmen of the old Tractarian school, he held no brief for Rome and was strongly critical of her system.) A Mr J. Hanchard published a *Sketch of the Life of Bishop King, with portrait*— the portrait supplied by a local Brigg photographer, and intended, by showing the new bishop in his eucharistic vestments, to make all good evangelical flesh creep.

It is easy enough, a hundred years on, to laugh at such petty sniping in print. But in 1885 religion was a much more dominant force in the life of the nation, and religious controversy was apt to be not only serious, but sustained and deadly. The conservative country districts, like the broad acres of Lincolnshire, were specially susceptible to anti-Roman hysteria. Perhaps today only Northern Ireland can give us a yardstick to gauge the depth and virulence of Victorian anti-Catholicism. It was hydra-headed, ancestral, subliminal; a compound of old, unhappy, far-off things, and battles not so very long ago. It drew on folk memories of Bloody Mary and Foxe's *Book of Martyrs*; Gunpowder Treason and Plot; the Catholic Irish threat during the Civil War; James II; and the Gordon Riots. In its nineteenth-century phase it had been fuelled by the Oxford Movement, the Catholic Revival in the Church of England, which had brought out the 'No Popery' banners with a vengeance. It was powerful and touchy and bore down reason and good sense. A cultivated scientist like Philip Gosse, who was also a member of the Plymouth Brethren, was so imbued with it that he could be prevailed on to buy from a Spanish onion-seller, whose cry was, 'Here's your rope, to hang the Pope, and a pennorth of cheese to choke him'. 'You are a Catholic, sir!' exclaimed the lady who saw the architect Pugin cross himself in a railway compartment; 'Guard, let me out—I must get into another carriage!' Around 1870, Sir Arthur Quiller-Couch recalled, his father, the local doctor, had imported into Bodmin a handful of Roman Catholic nurses to help in a scarlet fever epidemic. They came as 'Sisters of Mercy', but the scarlet fever epidemic paled before the hysteria provoked by the Scarlet Woman : 'At once there arose an outcry that he was importing Papacy and (on the bye) that the very garb of these sisters was enough to frighten the sick into their graves.'[18] It may all seem quaintly comic now; it did not seem so then, and a moment's reflection on the tragedy of Northern Ireland today should make us realize just what a potently destructive force 'No Popery' can be.

Lincolnshire in 1885, at the level of Protestant folk-religion, differed little from Cornwall in 1870. Both regions had been soaked in the Methodist Revival, and Lincoln was well known as a Low Church diocese. The outlook was not exactly rosy for a High Church bishop. When Scott Holland rejoiced that King's appointment would mean 'a S. Francis de Sales at Lincoln', he may have spoken more wisely than he knew. De Sales' winning gentleness and pastoral zeal both remind us of King; and their situations were not dissimilar either. De Sales was a Catholic bishop 'in the regions of the unbelievers', set to care for the diocese of Annecy in which the city of Geneva lay. He applied himself—with notable success—to the formidable task of winning back the people of this Calvinist stronghold to the Roman obedience. King's task in the diocese of Lincoln was hardly less testing. He set himself the aim, from the first, of winning over Nonconformists—and they were thick on the ground—to the Anglican Church. He had also to win many of his own Church people—Low Churchmen and Evangelicals—to accept the pastoral rule of a vigorous High Churchman.

King not only never masked the fact that he was a strong High Churchman. (That would have been difficult anyway, with the Cuddesdon label attached to his record.) He placarded the fact before all eyes by appearing in eucharistic vestments—still comparatively rare—and by wearing a mitre of striking size and beauty. He was indeed the first bishop to wear a mitre since the Reformation. He was no self-conscious trend-setter, but the mitre having been given him he duly wore it. He used often to recall with delight the conversation of two old Lincolnshire farm labourers on first seeing him accoutred in a mitre. 'That there hat on 'is 'ed do look exactly like a bee-house,' said one. 'Ah,' replied the other, 'but 'tis all sweetness as comes out of 'im.' Not everyone was so engagingly tolerant as the two old men. To many the mitre was a red rag to a bull, and it may be, as Owen Chadwick suggests, that King's decision to wear it when friends gave it only underlines his lack of political sense and worldly wisdom. 'Hitherto bishops had mitres on their spoons, their arms, their writing paper, their carriage-doors, their coffins. But never since the Reformation had a bishop of the Church of England worn a mitre upon his head.'[19] King, then, was an innovator; and though over half his clergy expressed a wish that he should wear it for confirmations in the first nine months of 1886, they did not necessarily speak for their people. King's goodness and pastoral concern disarmed much of the opposition, but not all by any means, and to the most discerning eyes the explosion, when it came, was not wholly unexpected.

Local opposition to his High Churchmanship was only one of the problems he faced when he came to Lincoln in his fifty-sixth year. His health had never been robust, and he looked older than his years. The local wiseacres, 'when first they saw his spare form and bent shoulders ... "reckoned" that the new Bishop "poor owd man, didn't look like being long for this world".'[20] They were wrong; he had another quarter-century to go. Though he had a pronounced stoop, and his hair was greying from the temples and his long side-whiskers were quite white, yet he was no old man. His eyes were keen and lively still, his brow relatively unfurrowed, his face eager and open. His main features all suggest great strength and determination of character—the long straight nose, the firm, well-set mouth, resolved without being grim; and the full, firm chin which carried its own message that his 'gentleness was not weakness, but restrained strength'.

He needed all his strength and courage as he squared up to the challenge of his sprawling rural diocese. One problem he had to contend with was the quality of the Lincolnshire clergy. He was warned before he entered the diocese that they were exhaustively divisible into three categories : those who were going out of their minds; those who had gone out of their minds; and those who had no minds to go out of. When we set that generalization beside the scholar-parsons of Lincolnshire in the eighteen-eighties, it looks frankly libellous. Men like the historian G. G. Perry of Waddington (the biographer of St Hugh), the mathematician, John Bond of Anderby, or the musician, Thomas Barker of Revesby, represented, it may be fairly said, the fine flower of the English parish clergy. Yet they were the exception, not the norm, and the average standard of the clergy was one of King's major concerns. He tried to tackle the problem at source, by striving to raise the standard of the men trained in the diocesan theological college, Bishop's Hostel, Lincoln. He also took remedial action by encouraging Clerical Reading Societies and by sponsoring annual clergy retreats for serious study.

Another difficulty he faced was the religious complexion of Lincolnshire as a stronghold of Nonconformity, and especially of Methodism in both its Primitive and Wesleyan forms. The returns from the parishes at his first visitation of the diocese brought home to him sharply the extent of the problem. 'Dissent! Dissent! Dissent!' was a constant theme, and to a bishop who saw his central task as being 'the Ministry of Reconciliation', it was a challenge he could not ignore. He told a friend that 'what he wanted to do in the diocese was to draw men to Christ, that they might be nearer to God, and nearer to each other in the unity of His Holy Church'.[21] He was not the first Bishop of Lincoln to try to win the Nonconformists back to the Church. His distinguished though rather absent-minded predecessor, Christopher Wordsworth, who was said to have one foot in heaven and the other in the third century, had tried it too. Unfortunately, his overtures tended to be rather brash and insensitive. He once urged the Wesleyan Methodist leader, William Arthur, to bring his people back into the Church of England, throwing in as an inducement, 'Would you not be glad to preach in Lincoln Cathedral?' Arthur answered drily, 'Well, I should be glad to preach in Lincoln Cathedral, and I should be glad to preach in a wheelbarrow.'[22] King as much as Wordsworth longed to bring Nonconformists back to the Church, but his sympathy and tact forbade any clumsy approach of this kind. He sympathized very deeply with the Nonconformists, and understood their feelings. The last few pages of his *Spiritual Letters* are taken up with scattered fragments of correspondence, crumbs gathered up by his pious editor, Randolph, so that nothing might be lost. The final one reads: 'I have always had a real sympathy for the Wesleyans and Primitives as people who wish to be good, but I do not believe we shall win them by giving away our Apostolical and Catholic position.'[23]

That sentence was written in August 1908, but it is typical both in the firmness of the Tractarian view which it expresses and in the genuinely ecumenical spirit which it breathes. King was quite prepared to acknowledge that the Church of England had in a real sense only itself to blame for the separation and growth of Methodism. In 1906 he confessed: 'I need hardly say that I have never had any harsh feeling towards Nonconformists, and, I might add, especially not towards Wesleyans and Primitive Methodists, because I have always felt that it was the want of spiritual life in the Church and brotherly love which led them to separate. The more we can draw near to Christ ourselves and fill ourselves with His Spirit, the greater power we shall have for unity. What we want is more *Christlike Christians.*'[24]

King's irenical attitude and sheer goodness of character earned him the respect and admiration of many Free Churchmen. Many Methodists went to hear him preach as he moved about the diocese; and, as George Russell emphasizes, 'Descendants of the men whom John Wesley had converted recognized that in their new bishop they had a man of God, who lived in prayer and preached Christ Crucified. . . . This was what they wanted, and his sermons were often punctuated by ejaculations of "Ah!" "Hallelujah!" and "Praise the Lord!" in the true fashion of the Methodists.'[25] The popular verdict on his simple, direct, evangelical preaching was: 'He's nowt but an owd Methody', and there is a profound sense, as I shall hope to show, in which Catholic and Evangelical meet in King. Yet it is perhaps not surprising that not even the ministry of this good and holy man was able to bring about a large-scale return of Nonconformists to the Church. There were no doubt many reasons for that fact, besides the basic, stubborn nature of the pre-ecumenical age in which he lived. There were deep-rooted historical and social factors separating Church and Chapel, which could not be overcome at the drop of a mitre, however saintly the head that wore it. Again, it was one thing for the bishop of the diocese to give a strong lead in the direction of church unity; quite another to translate that into practice at the parish level, where the shoe

81

really pinched. Finally, however attractive Catholic Anglicanism may be as a form of Christian faith and life—and it could hardly be more attractive than it was in Edward King—there remain elements and expressions of life in Christ which it does not comprehend, or at least did not in King's day. Spontaneity in worship, and the intimacy and freedom of the small, committed Christian fellowship, are merely two of these.

Yet King's ecumenism, though limited in visible results, did bear fruit. It softened attitudes and opened minds. In its strengths it has much to teach us in today's ecumenical scene. It began in penitence, and an acknowledgement of the failures of the Anglican Church. It sprang out of an equal commitment to truth and love. It insisted that the way for Christians to draw nearer to one another, was to come to the fountain-head and draw nearer to Christ himself. It would not be far-fetched, I believe, to trace the spirit of Edward King in the reactions of Lincolnshire Christians to the scheme for Anglican-Methodist unity in the 1960s. The enormously positive response in the Anglican Diocese and Methodist District owed much to the passionately ecumenical lead given by Bishop Kenneth Riches; and Kenneth Riches is a devout disciple of Edward King. Certainly it would have rejoiced the heart of King to see the widespread co-operation between Anglicans and other Christians in his diocese. He would surely see it as a partial fulfilment of his hopes and prayers, which are typified in the letter he sent in 1909 to the Wesleyan Methodist Conference, then meeting in Lincoln. On behalf of the cathedral clergy, he acknowledged that 'Although they and the Conference were not able in all points to see eye to eye, yet it would be unjust not to recognise the great work of those who had done so much for the religious life of their land in the days of their common neglect. They were one in their faith in Christ, and that He died for all—and if they took Him to be the type and example of their life, and got others to do so too, they would be more Christlike Christians. And the more they were like Him the nearer they would get to one another, and thus realise the Saviour's prayer that they all might be one.'[26]

Since many of the Methodists were found among the ranks of the agricultural labourers, for whom King had a special apostolic and caring concern, he had pastoral as well as ecumenical motives for going out to them. As he wrote to his friend R. L. Ottley, 'I am glad it is John Wesley's diocese. I shall try to be the Bishop of the Poor.'[27] King implies here a link between Wesley and the role of 'Bishop of the Poor'. It is simple fact that concern for the poor was always central to Wesley's ministry, and the text of the first open-air sermon he preached in England was, 'The Spirit of the Lord God is upon me; because the Lord hath anointed me to preach good tidings to the poor . . .' (Isaiah 61 : 1). King knew the same constraint, and in his Primary Visitation Charge of 1886 expressed his central aim as bishop: 'To bring home to the people, and especially to the poor, the blessings of the Church.'[28] It was a splendid declaration of intent; but how did it work out in practice, King's pastoral ideal of being 'Bishop of the Poor'?

One of his first acts as bishop expressed his pastoral concern in an acted parable. He did what Bishop Trevor Huddleston, living in a terraced house in the heart of his Stepney diocese, has done more recently: he came to live among his people. Since 1842 the bishops of Lincoln had lived in solitary splendour in a large and rambling palace at Riseholme, three miles outside the city. King was not happy about Riseholme, and wrote to a friend two months before he came to Lincoln, 'Just now my immediate difficulty is where to live—Riseholme, with my widowed Sister and all the children, or Lincoln alone. The second seems right if I can, if the Ecclesiastical Commissioners will let me sell Riseholme; but in my heart I cling to my sister and the children. However, by God's help, I hope to give myself first to the Diocese, and, if I can, live at Lincoln.'[29] In the event he did live at Lincoln, which was not only a large market town and cathedral city, but also a busy railway and engineering centre. He made his home in the Old Palace, the smaller, medieval home of the bishops, which had fallen into decay and was now restored for his use. The move brought him to the heart of his diocese and to the midst of his people. From his windows he could look out over the huddled roofs of the city climbing up the hill to the cathedral, in whose lee he lived. He could hear the factory buzzers and hooters calling his people to work, and the tramp of the men's boots in the streets close by. When he went into the engineering works, as he was regularly to do, he told the men he prayed for them as they went to work each day.

The great thing about the Old Palace was not that it was palatial—it was not—but that it was accessible. Living there Bishop King was at once at home to his clergy and people, readily available in the centre of the city. One reason why he put personal and family considerations aside and made the move was that, 'It wasn't every poor parson who had half-a-crown for a cab out to Riseholme.'[30] King was as concerned for the poor parsons as he was for the poor parishioners. Lincolnshire, as a major farming county, was severely hit by the Agricultural Depression in the late nineteenth century, and some of the poorer clergy, with large houses, large families, and small incomes, were in grievous straits. The daughter of the Revd John Hoult, Vicar of Scotton under King, has recalled for me the penury of some of their clerical neighbours. One clergyman, with a living worth only £90 a year, was so poor that the family 'lived off rabbits which came into the rectory garden'. King understood the needs of such men, and did his best to help them. He had carved over the door of the Old Palace a Latin text which was a reminder to him in all his goings out and in, and which might sum up his whole episcopate : 'Pascite gregem', 'Feed the flock'.

William Addison, in his *The English Country Parson*, speaks of King as 'the country parson's true father in God. Edward King might almost have been Chaucer's poor parson himself somehow become a bishop.'[31] It was true. The 'prince of the Church' image, which a bishop like Cosmo Gordon Lang radiated—he was not descended from the Medicis for nothing— held no meaning for King. He saw his office and his calling as pastoral through and through. On the very day of his consecration, we find him writing to a friend that he was looking forward to becoming 'a big curate in the diocese of Lincoln'.[32] Only he could have used that image of the bishop as a curate with an enlarged cure of souls. In many ways his personal life-style was still that of the curate of Wheatley he had been as a young man, when he had first begun to minister to the country poor. 'In his days at Wheatley, he had baffled a "little village girl, a most inveterate beggar," who complained that she had only one frock for Sundays and work-days, by saying, "Well, I have only this coat for Sundays and weekdays." A lady, who had been his neighbour at Cuddesdon, wrote on hearing of his appointment to Lincoln—"All new clothes now! No old boots hereafter for ever." '[33] Yet King as bishop, with his often shabby clothes and worn, patched boots, continued to be the despair of his friends and the spiritual brother of his country curates. They knew that when he prayed for them, aided by the book in which he kept a photograph of each of his clergy, he did so as one who understood the feeling of their infirmities.

King made himself pastorally accessible not only at the heart of his diocese, in Lincoln itself, but as far as possible throughout the Wolds, marsh, and fenland of the county. He was an incessant railway traveller, and managed to get into remote corners of the diocese that had hardly seen a bishop since the Middle Ages. He came to know the railwaymen well, and would always thank the driver and the guard at the end of a journey. He preached at special services for railwaymen in the cathedral, and after one sermon, in which he had described the demands and hazards peculiar to the railwayman's life, a veteran of the line commented, 'He might almost have been a railwayman himself'. The trains took him mainly to confirmations, though also to institutions of clergy, patronal festivals, harvest thanksgivings. He delighted most in the confirmations, when the ploughboys with their scrubbed faces and pomaded hair came to receive his blessing. His addresses on these occasions were simple, direct, and searching. Men and women who were confirmed by him as children are known to have remembered the kernel of his address seventy years later. 'If you want to be happy, you must learn to be good', was one of his favourite themes, which stuck like a burr in the memory of many who heard it.

There were a few sophisticates, among the farmers and professional people, who found him *too* simple and complained that his words were an insult to their intelligence. Yet that kind of criticism was rare. For the most part, not only the common people, but people in every walk of life, heard him gladly. He lit up his sermons with homely analogies which at once turned ears into eyes. In a Confirmation Address of 1888, we find him urging his young confirmands to 'put off' whatever is wrong in their lives: 'You must each of you think of something that you are going to put away. Sin is like a wheel set rolling down a hill, you may stop it at first, but not afterwards. Sin is also like a chain which is made up of little links, and if bound round your arms many times would be almost impossible to break.'[34]

What young man could easily forget the portrait of the village bravo which King draws in a sermon which sets before youngsters in the pride of early manhood the way of Samson or the way of Goliath: 'You know, a man can dedicate his strength either for God or against God. There was Goliath—he was a strong man, but he used his strength to defy God; and there was Samson, also a strong man, who used his strength on the side of God. And a young man that is strong and feels the tide of life rising in his veins, that knows all the wild joy of living, that is looked up to and admired by his companions in the village in which he lives—he may be a Goliath, and lead people, attracting them by his great strength, to defy and blaspheme God, and make the younger ones think it a fine thing to swear, a fine thing to drink, a fine thing not to go to Church, a fine thing to be rude—a strong young man may either, like Goliath, flout God in the face, or he may, like Samson, fight the Lord's battles, and show everyone in the village that it is not a cowardly thing to come to Church, that he is not ashamed to kneel and bow down before Almighty God, or to be kindly, and tender, and gentle to men and women, and to little children. A young man that has great strength may make that his gift. He knows he is looked up to for it. He may either set an example of defiance against God, or he may begin to cast his golden crown before the

Throne, and cherish in his heart the spirit of worship, of self-sacrifice, and of self-devotion.'[35]

This ability to get inside the hearts and minds of simple country people, to know the 'feel' of their lives from within, and to express the Faith in terms which were meaningful for them—this was King's great gift. He certainly was no great organizer or administrator. He admired Bishop Samuel Wilberforce, under whom he had served at Wheatley and Cuddesdon, as the New Model bishop. Wilberforce was a dynamo, training his clergy and organizing his diocese on a new pattern of streamlined efficiency. His energy seemed boundless, and he would think nothing of dashing off forty business letters in his own hand in the course of a single afternoon. He was a hard rider and good horseman, and his dash and vigour matched those of his mount. There is a strange appropriateness in the manner of his dying—his horse tripped, threw him headlong, and he died instantly. King admired Wilberforce's energy, self-sacrifice and dedication; but he was a bishop of a quite different kind. King once wrote to Wilberforce from Cuddesdon, on Boxing Day, 1866, and signed himself 'your most affectionate and obedient Servant', but added a postscript which expressed his frank concern that the bishop was driving himself far too hard : 'I hope you are really resting; you looked, not ill, but too *"driven"* when I saw you. I do wish you would promise to go in nothing but Parliamentary Trains for the whole of next year and be *shunted* every day for three hours, with no Post and no means of getting out—it would be the best thing for the Diocese and the Church.'[36] Wilberforce no doubt merely put this prescription down to King's whimsicality, and failed to take the serious point wrapped up in the banter. The fact was that Samuel's devoted concern for the Cause—the diocese, the clergy, the Church, the Faith— was apt to leave him too busy for individuals and their needs.

On one occasion the Bishop charmed the guests of the country house where he was staying, with his 'restless, eager stream of conversation', but quite failed to notice a young woman in great personal trouble who tried throughout the weekend to find an opportunity to broach it with him. In the end, she blurted out to him as he was mounting his horse to leave : 'My lord, are you always thus? Are you always so brilliant, and clever, and amusing? Is there any time when sorrowful people may speak to you about their soul's trouble?' Samuel's response was immediate and contrite. He 'started back in sudden amazement. His colour went from him. But then leaning forward he was his best self again, and in words inexpressibly touching he gave her to understand how in his position the world was ever about him, but gave her to understand that, though he might not have shown it, he was full of deep sympathy for such a case as hers. And then,' concludes the narrator of the story, 'he rode away.'[37] Samuel's response, though no doubt genuinely sympathetic, far from disproving the point the woman was trying to make to him, simply corroborates it. He was continually spurring his horse and riding off to the next important engagement, at some cost, inevitably, to his ministry to individuals.

King took a leaf out of Wilberforce's book in so far as he was eager to foster improved training for the clergy at Bishop's Hostel, and to encourage all kinds of diocesan societies and good works : the Communicants' Guild, the Men's Society, the Clerical Reading Societies, the Guild of St Barnabas for nurses, the Missionary Training College at Burgh-le-Marsh, and many others. Yet King never lost sight of the truth that the end and aim of all the multifarious aspects of diocesan life was to build individual men and women up in the truth and love of Christ. He had time for individuals and their needs; time to listen and notice, to respond and empathize. The Bishop of Rochester once remonstrated with Samuel Wilberforce, 'You have introduced such a system into the episcopate that one has time for nothing.'[38] King, who disliked what he called all this 'rushing about' by bishops, had time. He had time, for instance, for a sixteen-year-old apprentice photographer called Walter Lee, told off to get a picture of the Bishop after he had dedicated the new church of St Anne at Grantham on a May day in 1907. A lifetime later, Walter Lee recalled the occasion for *Lincolnshire Life*. He and his employer had rigged up their camera at the door of the parish room, hoping to catch King as he came there after the service. 'All was ready and after what seemed like an age a little procession appeared from around the corner. First came the Bishop's Chaplain with his crook, followed by the Bishop himself, again followed by a number of people. It was all very quiet and dignified. Alas, it appeared as though our luck had deserted us, for it had started to rain quite fast! The Bishop reached the doorway and my employer asked if he might take his photograph. The Chaplain said, "I am sorry, it's raining" and made a sign for the Bishop to go inside as quickly as possible. However, the Bishop turned, faced the camera and with that kindly smile for which he was so well known said, "I think I would like my photograph taken", and as he was standing quite still I squeezed the bulb, the air rushed up the rubber tube and the shutter opened and closed as it had done so many times before. Little did I realize that this time, at this very moment, I was helping to make the most sought after portrait of my career.'[39]

The photograph which Walter Lee took is, by all accounts, a speaking likeness of Edward King. It is the portrait reproduced by Randolph as the frontispiece to his edition of King's *Spiritual Letters*, and when King died it was printed in postcard form and circulated widely through the diocese. Copies of it are still treasured among the Lincolnshire people. King was in his seventy-eighth year, bowed with age, his hair now quite white. Yet there is the same marvellous combination of strength and tenderness in the face. It is the face of a man who has listened long and intently to the still, sad music of humanity, and who has yet retained his faith and hope. What the picture cannot show, and what we should never have known but for Walter Lee's memory, is that he is standing in the pouring rain in his splendid flowered cope, in deference to a little local photographer and his boy apprentice.

King was willing to turn his hand to any pastoral need or duty. He never stood on episcopal ceremony—after all, what was a bishop but a 'big curate', a man with an enlarged pastoral responsibility? So he would willingly do duty for the chaplain to the almshouses in St Anne's parish, Lincoln, and visit the elderly ladies who lived there. One of them in 1945 still looked back to his first visit to her, and recalled her embarrassment when he was about to pray with her. 'I am sorry, my Lord,' she apologized, 'but I haven't a hassock.' 'Never mind,' said King, 'the floor's good enough for me, and the pain in my knees will keep me humble.' A more costly pastoral duty he undertook was in Lincoln Castle gaol. Today, the old Castle gaol houses the County Record Office and its fine series of manuscripts, including many of King's own letters and papers. In his day, however, it was a grim prison, and only a stone's throw from the Old Palace where he lived. He had only to go through the cathedral Close, under Exchequergate arch, and across the cobbled Castle yard, to be in the prison. Early in 1887, a young fisherman from Grimsby, Richard ——, was condemned to death at Lincoln Assizes for the murder of his sweetheart in a lovers' quarrel. The chaplain to the gaol was inexperienced and distressed at having to minister to a man who was, from all report, completely brutalized. In the event, King relieved the chaplain of the duty and ministered to the young man himself. The murderer was young, uneducated—'as ignorant as a South Sea Islander', in King's words—with no knowledge of religion and very little understanding of right and wrong. 'He was simply a powerful animal,' as King told George Russell, 'and had acted on his animal instincts' in perpetrating this *crime passionnelle*. 'The Bishop set to work, and taught him the unseen realities of life and death, sin and forgiveness, from the Parable of the Prodigal Son. The youth was deeply moved, and the Bishop, having satisfied himself that he had been baptized, confirmed him, received his Confession, and prepared him for Holy Communion.'[40] King saw him daily for the last few weeks of his life. After wrestling with his conscience—because he thought the sentence just—and having consulted the trial Judge, King signed a petition for mercy on behalf of the boy. It was rejected by the Home Secretary, and the bishop was left to prepare the young man for his death. He celebrated the Eucharist in the death cell, and before the service took the youth by the hand and said, 'Let us say a little prayer to consecrate the hand which did the sad deed, before it holds the Body of the Lord.' King went to the scaffold with him, ministering to him until the hangman released the trap. He wrote to Russell a day or two later : 'It was a terrible privilege, but I am most thankful that I was allowed to be with the poor dear man. He was most beautiful; and his last (and first) Communion on Sunday morning put me to shame. I felt quite unworthy of him. How little the world knows of the inner life.'[41]

From then on, Edward King made a habit of visiting prisoners awaiting sentence of death in the gaol, and spent long periods with them in prayer and counselling. It was here perhaps that he was most profoundly 'the Bishop of the Poor', as he ministered the love of God in the valley of the shadow of death, to the condemned, the outcast, and the forsaken. George Russell is surely right when he makes the point that 'Such ministrations, from which far more robust men would have shrunk in horror, revealed that nerve of steel which God so often bestows on the gentlest of his saints.'[42]

CHAPTER SEVEN

Bishop on Trial

> The only thing I regret (sc. being cut out of his editorial for the *Guardian,* dealing with the trial of Bishop King) is a quotation I had prepared for the special benefit of the Dean of Wells. It is where Joubert says that one is easily deceived when one differs from poets about poetry or from the saints about religion.
>
> *D. C. Lathbury to Henry Liddon*, 5 March 1889[1]

I FIRST 'met' Edward King, so to say, in 1962, while taking part in a conference at the Old Palace, Lincoln, his home for twenty-five years. Today it is the Diocesan Retreat House and Conference Centre, a quiet and hospitable house, which still retains something of the savour of King's presence. The famous peacocks he had on his lawn have of course gone. So too has his ample library. But the chapel he made out of a ruinous wing of the medieval palace is still in use, the chapel for which his old friend William Bright wrote the eucharistic hymn, 'And now, O Father, mindful of the love', which was sung at the consecration. There remain too portraits and engravings of King. Coming down the main stairs of the house, on the first evening of my stay, I was struck by the subject of a large engraving on the staircase wall. It was entitled 'The Lincoln Judgement' and showed King, in full canonicals, appearing for trial before the Archbishop of Canterbury and six other bishops.

Since bishops do not come up for trial every day of the week, I was arrested by the picture. As soon as I reached home after the conference, I made a bee-line for my *Oxford Dictionary of the Christian Church*, which in its cool, laconic way gave me the gist of the story which the picture told. Under 'Lincoln Judgement', I read: 'The Judgement, given in 1890 by E. W. Benson, Archbishop of Canterbury, upon the com-

93

plaints made two years before by the Church Association against Edward King, Bishop of Lincoln, for consecrating the Eucharist in the eastward position, having lighted candles on the Altar, mixing water and wine in the Chalice, allowing the Agnus Dei to be sung after the Consecration, absolving and blessing with the sign of the Cross, and taking the ablutions of the sacred vessels. The Judgement upheld the Bishop in the main, but ordered that the Chalice must be mixed, if at all, before the service, that the manual acts of consecration must be visible to the people, and that the sign of the Cross may not be used. The Judgement was notable in that it ignored previous decisions of the secular courts and the Judicial Committee of the Privy Council. . . .' The Judgement was also notable, as I was to discover, because it almost broke King's heart. The terse factual survey of the *Dictionary* cannot convey anything of the strain he underwent: the trial by publicity, for a man who was by nature modest and retiring; the four years' agony and uncertainty of the hearings, the Judgement, and the Appeal, which was not determined until 1892; the burden of coping with the work of his diocese at the same time as being the accused in a *cause célèbre*.

How was it, then, that King, the gentlest of men, should have become—apart from one dubious precedent—the only Anglican bishop since the Reformation to be tried in the Archbishop of Canterbury's own court of special jurisdiction? It was on ritual charges that King was tried, and to understand the growth of a more elaborate ritual in the Victorian Church, there are one or two prime points to be grasped. The first concerns the Catholic Revival in the Church of England, stemming from the Oxford Movement and the work of the great Tractarians. That movement was at first concerned with ritual little if at all. Pusey once admitted that he had never even seen a chasuble; and as late as 1873 at Christ Church, Oxford, a traditional Tractarian stronghold, 'much of the old simplicity prevailed. Canon Pusey and Canon King knelt opposite each other at the ends of the Altar; we still received the Holy Communion kneeling in our places in the body of the church', as Luke Paget

recalled of his undergraduate days.[2] The High Church Movement, in its original and formative phase, was certainly not
obsessed with ritual. If we may borrow a twentieth-century
slogan, its watchword was in essence, 'Let the Church be the
Church!' It brought with it a renewal and deepening of
theology, especially in the realm of Church, Ministry and Sacraments. It also issued in a renewal of discipline, holiness and
spirituality. Like the Puritan Movement of the seventeenth
century, and the Evangelical Revival of the eighteenth, it was a
call to Christianity in earnest, and a more devoted following of
the way of discipleship.

In the second phase of the Movement, however, and especially
among some of its younger exponents, the place of ritual bulked
much larger. Colour, lights, movement, processions, chants,
incense, statues, paintings, began to enrich—opponents said
desecrate—the worship of numerous Anglo-Catholic churches.
It would be easy to assume in our age, when worship and social
concern have often been polarized, that the ritualists were
diverting the energies of churchmen from the broad highway of
social responsibility into a liturgical cul-de-sac. Nothing could
have been further from the truth. The leading London ritualists
were also the great slum priests, men with a passionate social
concern for the poor and oppressed. Clergymen like Charles
Lowder of St Peter's, London Docks, or A. H. Mackonochie of
St Alban's, Holborn, with a devotion centred in the eucharist,
saw very clearly the blasphemy of sharing bread in church, and
being content with a form of society which allowed men to rob
one another of their daily bread outside. For these men, there
was no conflict between ritual and social concern; each implied
the other. For them one aspect of ritual was its power, through
eye-gate as well as ear-gate, to make religion real to the poor
and illiterate.

There is no denying, however, that the introduction of a
more advanced ritual into a parish church often caused conflict.
Where, as in many of the large city parishes, a church had been
newly built to cope with increased population, and where there
was no established tradition to break with, there might be no

internal dissension. But where ritual changes took place within a settled congregation, the odds on trouble were high. The hackles of the No Popery brigade were sure to rise. There might be physical violence, blasphemous abuse and disruption of services, as in the notorious disturbances at St George's in the East, where groups of strong young men formed themselves into a bodyguard for the vicar. There might be legal action taken against the innovating clergyman.

The Public Worship Regulation Act of 1874 was an attempt by statute to bring more uniformity into the ritual arrangements of Anglican churches. It did not change the law of ritual, which continued to be governed by the rubrics of the Book of Common Prayer. Rather, it tried to put teeth into the ecclesiastical courts and ensure their more effective working. In the event it failed to bring the most convinced and determined ritualist clergy to heel, because many of them would not recognize the right of the courts, operating under a secular statute, to regulate the worshipping life of Christ's Church. Five of such men, rather than plead before such courts, went to gaol, one of them—the Revd S. F. Green of St John's, Miles Platting, Manchester—for twenty months. Many others would almost certainly have been imprisoned but for the fact that their Bishop used his veto to prevent a prosecution, when he saw that the result of a trial would be to send a conscientious clergyman to gaol. The charges against these men were sometimes brought on the initiative of a parishioner, sometimes at the instance of an ultra-Protestant group like the Church Association, which would send its agents into Anglo-Catholic services in order to gain evidence for a prosecution. It was the Church Association which had been lurking in the wings and threatening to protest at Edward King's confirmation of election as Bishop of Lincoln. They had held their fire then. Three years later they let fly, and by their action brought him to face trial before Archbishop Benson.

Before we turn to the Lincoln Judgement, we must set the scene in a little more detail. Until 1963, the final court of appeal in ecclesiastical cases was the Judicial Committee of the Privy Council. By 1889, when King stood trial, many people, Churchmen and non-Churchmen, had come to question whether in fact the Judicial Committee was the proper place in which to settle conscientious differences of doctrine, liturgy and worship. The lawyers were often embarrassed at being asked to pronounce on such matters. They were judges, not canonists, and fewer and fewer of them had been trained in civil or ecclesiastical law. Again, though the Book of Common Prayer was a legal document and its usages enforceable in the courts, yet it was often extremely difficult to discern what the rubrics of the Prayer Book allowed, and, at points where latitude was clearly permitted, what were the limits of Anglican usage and tradition. What all this added up to in many Victorian minds was that it was high time the Church of England put its own worshipping house in order, and found means of deciding controverted matters of liturgy and worship without having recourse to the state courts. One final piece of background, and then we may turn to the Bishop of Lincoln's case. As we have seen, after the Public Worship Regulation Act of 1874, the bishops increasingly used their veto to prevent ritualist clergymen from being tried, condemned, and sent to prison. Their blocking action, especially where it sprang from High Church sympathies with the accused, opened up the obvious possibility that proceedings might be taken by ultra-Protestant groups against the bishop himself. That is partly what happened in the case of Edward King.

In the autumn of 1886, a churchwarden of Clee-cum-Cleethorpes, Mr Ernest de Lacy Read, brought charges of ritualism against his rector, a notable High Churchman, J. P. Benson. Bishop King used his veto to bar the prosecution, but at the same time brought persuasion to bear on Benson to moderate his practice. Benson agreed to revert to the simpler, traditional ritual of communion once a month. Read, who was a local solicitor, decided to take the matter further, and appealed against King's decision to the Archbishop of Canterbury. The Primate refused, and a little more than eighteen months later Read, in concert with the Church Association, decided to indict King himself. On 22 June 1888, the Church Association petitioned Archbishop Benson to try Bishop King for ritual acts contrary

97

to the Prayer Book which he had committed at Communion services held at the Cathedral (4 December 1887) and at the little church of St Peter-at-Gowts in Lincoln High Street (18 December 1887).

Benson was placed in a serious dilemma by the action of the Church Association. If he refused to act in the matter, he ran the risk of being ordered to act by the Judicial Committee, and he would seem to be running away from his responsibilities. On the other hand, if he heard the case and gave a judgement, there was a risk that the Church Association might appeal against his decision and have it overruled by the Judicial Committee of the Privy Council. There would then be the makings of a grave rift between Church and State. In deciding to convene his court and try King, Benson hoped no doubt to draw the sting of the reproach that the Church lacked convincing leadership in matters of worship. He hoped too that a clear lead from Lambeth might bring a measure of peace and unity to a sadly divided Church. He was fortified in his decision to proceed to a hearing by the ruling of the Judicial Committee, which he consulted, that he had legal jurisdiction in such a case.

Archbishop Benson convened his special court in the Library of Lambeth Palace. He summoned six bishops of the southern province to act as assessors in the trial, though he alone gave judgement. At least one of the assessors, the monumentally learned historian, Bishop Stubbs of Oxford, shared Dean Church's reservations about the composition and standing of the court. Church called the one precedent for it 'fishy'; Stubbs could be heard during the trial muttering under his breath, 'This is not a court; it is an Archbishop sitting in his Library.' King himself, fortified by the opinion of both lawyers and theologians, made a firm and courteous protest at the beginning of the trial. He urged that the law and custom of the Church required that the assessors should have been, not six bishops handpicked by Archbishop Benson, but all the bishops of the southern province. In other words, he should have been tried before all his peers, assembled as a full gathering of comprovincials.

We have already glanced at the ritual charges on which King was tried. Some contemporaries no doubt dismissed the whole trial as a colossal irrelevance to the human tragedy—rather as Thomas Hardy exclaims in *Jude the Obscure* : 'They are two clergymen of different views, arguing about the eastward position. Good God—the eastward position and all creation groaning.' So King was dismissed in some fashionable circles as 'a narrow but well-meaning formalist'[3]—a description which is about as far from King's spirit as one can easily get in five words. It is important to get certain facts straight. King was not 'arguing about the eastward position'. He was being prosecuted for following the normal pattern of worship at St Peter-at-Gowts. The particular ritual customs he was on trial for were in fact being practised, without harm or complaint, in many English parish churches at this time. They were in fact 'exceedingly moderate customs, more moderate (as was observed) than were practised in London churches attended by the prime minister and the Prince of Wales'.[4] The charges did not include what were the main issues of controversy at the time—the use of incense, eucharistic vestments, statues in the churches.

Hardy's testy remark—'Good God—the eastward position and all creation groaning'—is understandable as spoken of pernickety High Churchmen arguing over minutiae of ritual, magnified out of all proportion to their importance. King was not of that breed; and moreover, in a curious way, Hardy's dismissory phrase brings out the truth that ritual practice may have profound doctrinal significance. Ironically, Hardy's words about the eastward position contain unconscious echoes of the central Christian paradox. To face the east is to look to Jerusalem, to Calvary, to the Risen Lord. It is precisely there that the reconciling action of the 'Good God' is to be seen, cosmic in scale and power, alone able to heal the groaning of all creation. King, in facing east to consecrate; in mixing wine and water in the chalice (symbol of the blood and water which the spear-thrust drew from Christ's side); in allowing the 'Lamb of God who takest away the sins of the world...' to be sung after consecration; in cleansing the vessels and consuming the remains of the consecrated elements; was acting doctrinally as well as liturgically. He was using ritual to help make clear two truths. First, the sacrament was anchored in history, the history of Jesus, crucified and risen. Second, that same Jesus, in all His divine humanity, was really, personally, sacramentally present in the Eucharist.

The remaining charges against him—having lighted candles on the altar, and using the sign of the cross to absolve and bless —no doubt have a more muted theological significance. Certainly they do not relate so closely to the specific meaning of the Eucharist. The sign of the cross points up the Christian concern with history rather than timeless truth. The candles, lit even in daylight, are a sign and token of what an old Lincolnshire labourer described, to King's delight, as 'a yon-side religion'.

A great volume of prayer and concern and support welled up around King during the trial. The English Church Union, a High Church group with many local branches, was staunch in its support. At Ely Theological College, the Logbook records under 4 February 1890 : 'Today being fixed for the resumption of the trial of the Bishop of Lincoln at Lambeth, the Holy Eucharist was offered in chapel with the special intention of interceding that God would over-rule the trial for His greater glory and the good of His Church.'[5] Close friends like Sub-dean and Mrs Clements at Lincoln were a tower of strength to him. He wrote to Mrs Clements, who had just sent him a bunch of violets, on Christmas Eve, 1889 : 'I am sure I owe you, with others, more than I can say for the support you have gained for me through Prayer during this past year; for I have been most mercifully upheld with hardly any suffering, though of course the special burden is a great and unexpected one in addition to the necessary care of the Episcopate. Still, I hope and think, I see the Hand of God in this, working for the good of the Church of England, and so I trust a blessing will come to our own Diocese in time. Something of the sort, I think, was probably necessary, and it is a most wonderful mercy that it has come in a way which causes no ill-feeling towards any one and has not hindered the general work of the Diocese. I can never forget the loyalty and kindness which I have received during the last year.'[6]

It is said that King was the most popular man in Lincolnshire during the period of the trial. Certainly he won large support in the diocese, both from Anglicans and from those outside the Church of England. Petitions on his behalf were widely signed; monies were raised to help defray his legal expenses; many prayers were offered on his behalf. The proceedings opened at Lambeth on a miserably cold day, 12 February 1889. The six episcopal assessors wore their scarlet robes; King wore a fur-lined coat given him by his friend, H. O. Wakeman, the Oxford historian. On the same day King sent a letter to each incumbent in the Lincoln diocese. It contained the opening statement he had made before the Archbishop and the plea he had entered against the composition of the court. It ended with a personal word of explanation : 'I may add, to avoid misconception, that it is not, and it has never been, my desire to enforce any un-accustomed observance on an unwilling congregation; but my hope now is that this prosecution may, in God's providence, be so overruled as ultimately to promote the peace of the Church by leading to some authoritative declaration of toleration for certain details of ritual observance, in regard to which I believe that they are either in direct accordance with the letter of the Prayer Book, or at the least in loyal and perfect harmony with the mind of the Church of England. Asking for your prayers that I may know and do our Divine Master's Will in all things, I am, my dear Brother, Yours sincerely, EDWARD LINCOLN.' [7]

In the event, when the long-awaited decision was given from Lambeth, on 21 November 1890, Archbishop Benson decided substantially in King's favour. He upheld him in all his ritual acts save two. King loyally accepted his ruling that the manual acts of consecration must be visible to the people, and that the sign of the cross should not be used. Benson's long and learned judgement was the fruit of much study in liturgical history. It was a genuine attempt to provide liturgical guide-lines based not on legal precedents of the Judicial Committee of the Privy Council, but on the Prayer Book rubrics and on the traditional practice and usage of the Church. In its search for precedent and tradition it took for granted the continuity of the English Church across the great divide of the Reformation, which gave a boost to the morale of the High Churchmen. Benson's assertion of spiritual independence for the Church in ordering its own worshipping life earned the Judgement a splendid tribute from a great Tractarian, Dean R. W. Church of St Paul's. Church, who was then in his last illness, roused himself to greet the decision as 'The most courageous thing that has come from Lambeth for the last two hundred years'.[8]

King readily accepted the Judgement, and in a letter to Sub-dean Clements—5 December 1890—wrote: 'On the whole, Church-people are, I think, thankful for the Judgement. I am, myself, very thankful for the true Principles on which it has been based . . . I am no Ritualist, as you know; but, where the doctrine is sound, I rejoice that our simpler (and, I believe, often better and holier) brethren may have the help which sound and sight may be to true devotion. . . .'[9] The Church Association appealed to the Judicial Committee against the Judgement, and the appeal was rejected. Had it gone the other way, King's letters show clearly that he would not have accepted a ruling of the secular court which countermanded the Archbishop's ruling in a court spiritual. After the Judicial Committee had upheld the Judgement, on 2 August 1892, King wrote to his chaplain on 5 December: 'I am very thankful that we have been spared a great collision between Church and State. I do not think the Country is ready for it, and it would have split the Diocese in two. Personally too I am thankful that the strain of the last three years has been removed as it was becoming almost too much for my strength. But God knows and most mercifully relieves. Deo gratias!'[10] As Owen Chadwick judiciously observes: 'In the tension of the time a truculent Bishop of Lincoln could have split the Church of England into two. It was a mercy for the established Church that the new Bishop of Lincoln was a man without truculence.'[11]

The trial also effectively broke the back of the series of prosecutions for ritualism which had been such a bitter part of the Victorian religious scene. Men came to see that the law was a crude blunt instrument for dealing with such subtle and delicate matters as the pattern of a people's prayers. Ritualism did not cease, but there was a growth of tolerance and understanding. Yet all this was not without great cost to King himself. Through the long-drawn out agony of the accusation, the hearing, the trial, the judgement and the appeal, King was subject to constant strain. His spirituality, with its stress on maintaining a 'gentle calmness' and 'going quietly and steadily on', was put to the most searing test. He came through it, but it marked him for the rest of his life. The Lincolnshire people reckoned that the burden of these years 'broke him up a lot', and King's letters suggest that he would not have dissented from that view. On 14 August 1889, he wrote to Bramley his chaplain, 'Pardon this letter which is all about myself. Of course one could not expect to engage in a war without some losses—when it is all over, I hope the good will prevail. One begins to feel that it is wise to discharge soldiers at *sixty*, or *before*! . . .'[12] King was just a few months away from his sixtieth birthday when he wrote that, and the strain was obviously telling. When it was all over, on 30 December 1892, he wrote to Clements: 'All the publicity of the last four years has been most unexpected and painful to me. I trust it will be overruled for good. If it please God, I shall be thankful to live on and work. I have, indeed, very, very much to be thankful for, and among my many Blessings I shall always remember your forbearing, helpful kindness. I think this week has been one of the happiest I have spent for some years, *Deo Gratias*.'[13]

He did live on and work, for another eighteen years after 1892, which brought an end to his time of troubles. The words King used to round off this whole harrowing episode, we may write over the rest of his life, and its ending in faith and love: *Deo gratias.*

CHAPTER EIGHT

'Thy gentleness hath made me great'

> All his life he had been making doctrine a simple, homely fact; as if he were continually lighting fires in magnificent but sometimes chilly rooms. 'Don't you want to get Church words out of church?' he had written, 'they have got too closely associated with their surroundings; they have lost their urging clearness, their homely, natural, every-day meaning,' or again, 'Don't you long for human Christians and Christian humans?'
>
> *Elma K. Paget, writing of her husband, Luke Paget, a disciple of Edward King*

> He was the most saintly of men, and the most human of saints.
>
> *Archbishop C. G. Lang on Edward King*

'To be "meek and lowly in heart" is still the brightest glory of a Bishop.' 'I shall continue on my way and according to my own temperament. Humility, simplicity, fidelity to the Gospel in word and works, with unfaltering gentleness, inexhaustible patience and fatherly and insatiable enthusiasm for the welfare of souls.' 'St Francis de Sales is my great teacher. Oh if I could really be like him, in everything!' In these quotations, and in the invocation of that gentle saint, Francis de Sales, we are very close to the spirit of Edward King. It is de Sales who writes, 'Nothing is so strong as gentleness—nothing so loving and gentle as strength'.[1] King might have written that sentence, for it typifies his life; as indeed he might substantially have written the opening sentences of this chapter, which are in fact all culled from Pope John XXIII's *Journal*.[2] In the two men, there are so many likenesses: their humble simplicity, their realization that the real thing in the ministry—and the episcopate—is the foot-washing; their devotion to the poor; their gentleness of spirit, which has yet a toughness and resilience which gets things done. Both men see high office in the Church as fundamentally *diakonia*, ministry, service. King is the 'big curate' in Lincoln diocese; John XXIII, in fact as well as in title, servant of the servants of God, and a working Bishop of Rome, visiting the parishes, hospitals, prisons of his diocese.

Yet, though the parallel is suggestive and might be pursued at far greater length, though it may serve to bring out the catholicity of the saints, it is not helpful if it tends to remove King from his English setting. Francis de Sales, John XXIII and Edward King may well be, in character and Christ-likeness, blood-brothers. In spirituality, however, they represent different traditions, and to understand them even a little we must place them each in his distinctive setting. King I would see as a classic example of what Martin Thornton calls 'the English School of Spirituality : sane, wise, ancient, modern, sound, and simple; with roots in the New Testament and the Fathers'.[3] The great names here are those of St Anselm, Julian of Norwich, Margery Kempe of Lynn, George Herbert, John Donne, Nicholas Ferrar of Little Gidding. The characteristics of this English School are unitive and concerned with wholeness. Its exponents are eager not to put asunder what God has joined together : head and heart, doctrine and devotion, worship and daily life, dogma and pastoral warmth and love of souls. They want, like Luke Paget, to get 'Church words out of church' so that they may recover their 'homely, natural every-day meaning'. Its ethos is a domestic one, the family life of the people of God; and its marks are 'freedom', 'homeliness' and 'pastoral warmth'.[4] The land which Martin Thornton describes here is surely King country, and we recognize among the landmarks Cuddesdon, the Christ Church 'Bethel', and the whole 'bishopric of love' which was King's work at Lincoln.

If the classic English tradition of spirituality insists on the marriage of the homely and the holy, it is only to transpose that thought into a higher theological key to see grace as perfecting nature rather than destroying it. This truth is clearly seen in the life and sanctity of another examplar of the English tradition, Aelred, the twelfth-century Abbot of Rievaulx. He presided over that great Yorkshire house in the palmy days when it had six hundred choir monks and lay brothers within its sheltering walls. In his 'distinctively English' pattern of Christian living, A. M. Allchin singles out his 'love for history . . . love for Scripture, disinclination for speculative and systematic theology. There is the wonderful sense of pastoral responsibility, which shines out in many of his writings, and which made the Abbey of Rievaulx a place where both strong and weak could find life under his gentle but discerning guidance. Above all there is the conviction which his whole life and teaching expresses, that grace does not overthrow nature, but fulfils and perfects it.'[5]

King's life undoubtedly expressed the same truth. He would have joyfully assented to Von Hügel's aphorism that 'Grace is not the cuckoo, which drives all other birds out of the nest'. In the last sermon he preached at Christ Church before leaving Oxford in 1885, King related this doctrine of grace to the purpose of the Incarnation. He rejoiced that 'by God's great goodness we Christians can look up higher than our own nature, for we have seen His nature descend, not to destroy, but to take up humanity into the Godhead.'[6] There is no doubt that in Edward King nature and grace cohered and reinforced one another in a way that made for a simple and massive integrity of character. Let Scott Holland, perhaps the most articulate and sensitive of all King's friends, express it in his own inimitable way : 'Throughout, one was conscious of this rounded normality. There was nothing in him one-sided, or excessive, or unbalanced . . . Everything hung together. Everything befitted. . . . His natural manhood always found itself, in whatever he did : and showed itself complete and distinctive. And Grace had so intimately mingled with his nature that it was all of one piece. Grace itself had become natural. Who could say which was which? Was it all Grace? Was it all nature? Was it not all both? Anyhow, the whole man moved altogether, in every word and act. There were no separate compartments; and no disturbing reserves . . . so that the impact he made upon one was absolutely simple and undivided. The central spirit tingled in every pressure of the hand, in every turn of the voice, in every gleam of the eye. You had the whole of him, whenever you touched him. That was one of the unique delights of his companionship.' Owen Chadwick glosses those words to bring out the strange double impact King made on other people. 'The Christian life, he made them feel, was supernatural, yes; but not strange, or unnatural, or forced, or inhuman, or narrow. This was what man was born for. It was normality itself. It was balanced, sane, unwarped. It was man as he ought to be.'[8]

Together with this union of the holy and the homely, the supernatural and the natural life, it is possible to see in King an amalgam of what are often thought to be disparate and opposed traditions, the Catholic and the Evangelical. It was Pusey who once said, 'I love the Evangelicals, because they love our Lord'; and it is often overlooked that there are real affinities between the Tractarians and those who stand in the Evangelical tradition. Liddon 'insisted . . . on the Evangelical element there is in all true Churchmanship', and advised Luke Paget, a High Churchman beginning his ministry in an Evangelical parish (St Pancras), 'to read the great Evangelical Divines' like Wilberforce and Philip Doddridge, and to preach an opening course of sermons on Sin, Atonement, Grace, Justification and Sanctification.[9] Bramwell Booth of the Salvation Army records how Liddon himself would attend 'some of my weekly Holiness Meetings in Whitechapel, where he appeared much at home, taking a hearty share in the singing and evidently stirred by the testimonies'.[10] Similarly King shared much common ground with the Evangelicals. His catholicity did not want to repudiate much of what they stood for, but to set it in a wider and fuller context of faith and practice. His characteristic way of speaking of Jesus was as 'Saviour', and two who heard him preach often held that the motto of all his sermons could well be, 'He preached Christ to them'. No wonder that many Wesleyans and Primitives in his diocese, hearing him preach, acknowledged, 'He's nowt but an old Methody'.

It is a German scholar, Dieter Voll, with perhaps an outsider's sharper view of the English religious scene, who has written, in *Catholic Evangelicalism*, of the acceptance of Evangelical traditions by the Oxford Movement in the later nineteenth century. There is a clear sense in which King is an Evangelical Catholic, and, as Bernard Manning reminded us thirty years ago, it sometimes happens that 'In piety . . . extremes agree : Catholic and Evangelical meet . . . at the Cross'.[11] Manning the historian effectively links the pre-Reformation altar of the Five Wounds of Christ at Bardney Abbey, Lincolnshire, with the spirituality of the Charles Wesley hymns sung by the eighteenth-century Methodist farm-labourers of Bardney, with their lines like,

> Five bleeding wounds He bears,
> Received on Calvary;
> They pour effectual prayers,
> They strongly speak for me . . .[12]

More recently, Dr Michael Ramsey, the then Archbishop of Canterbury, made a strikingly similar point in a sermon he preached at the Nottingham Faith and Order Conference of 1964. He suggested that at the deepest levels of the life of faith, in devotion and spirituality, even the most widely separated ecclesiastical traditions may find themselves astonishingly close together : 'In a depth below doctrinal thought and structure, heart speaks to heart. May there not be, to give another instance, a similar apartness in the realm of thought and nearness in the depth of religious meaning in the case of some of the cleavages about faith, justification and the sacraments? I came across recently this remark in the memoirs of the late Father Waggett of Cowley. "There is no better expression of exactly what we mean by the sacrifice of the Mass than the hymn *Rock of Ages*." '[13]

Lest it be thought that Edward King was singular in combining Catholic and Evangelical elements in his piety, we may glance at a distinguished parish priest in the Tractarian tradition who died as recently as 1961, Canon Peter Green of Manchester. He was utterly devoted to the work of a parish priest, and must have set a record for the number of bishoprics he declined. His biographer says of him : 'First, he was a convinced Tractarian, which meant that while he had no intention of introducing High Church practices, he was determined to build up his people on sound

Catholic teaching ... Secondly, he was himself a deeply converted man, and in that sense a convinced Evangelical. The only kind of religion he considered worth having was a "vital religion", the religion of first-hand experience."[14] Unlike Green, King did introduce some 'High Church practices'—he was the first Anglican bishop since the Reformation to wear vestments, for example. Yet he was no rabid ritualist. His simplicity of character and pastoral concern ruled that out. In essence he combined the same 'sound Catholic teaching' and vital evangelical religion as Peter Green, who served his curacy under King's old friend E. S. Talbot, did later.

For King, as for Green, the *fulness* of the Catholic Faith was what mattered. There is in these men a concern for coherence, wholeness, proportion in life and teaching. King's views of things were long and wide and deep, comprehensive and inclusive. 'Never drop *anyone*', he would advise, in the matter of friendships. He urged his clergy to see the studies of their working life of forty or fifty years as a whole, and plan them out accordingly: 'Every priest ought to have a plan of study all through his life'.[15] This concern for wholeness and consistency, harmony and proportion, runs through his whole approach to Christian truth and life. In his Pastoral Lectures, he would urge his ordinands: 'Observe if the Church has provoked schism (and she has) by the deficiencies of her teaching and practice, yet the Church is capable of offering all the elements of truth claimed by the sects, and in truer proportion: it is this that they need. Dissent is a loss of proportion, a loss of harmony.'[16] To Francis Paget, no mean judge, King was a choice example of just this quality of 'proportion in teaching', as he wrote to James Adderley in 1887: 'I do think *proportion* in teaching is essential to the presentation of the truth: and that every year I get to trust more deeply and thankfully and entirely those who maintain above all the true proportion between the things that are welcome & the things that are unwelcome, the things that make people look pleasant & the things that make them look puzzled or annoyed, the things that get applause & the things that get silence or hisses.—I mean men like the Bishop of Lincoln and the Dean of St. Paul's, and Gore.—It is a rare strength that grows in them.'[17]

Certainly, no man set more store by the Bible and preaching than King. No one taught more clearly from the Scriptures the saving and sanctifying power of Christ. Yet with that powerful evangelical drive there went also King's championship of the centrality of the Eucharist in Christian faith and life, of auricular confession, of monastic vows and the renewal of the religious life in the Anglican Church. Popular Protestantism might scream that these were irreconcilable elements; the fact remains that they *were* reconciled in King's way of following Christ.

In the space that remains we shall examine five marks of that distinctive union of nature and grace which was expressed in King's Evangelical Catholicism: quietness, joy, sympathy, simplicity, and hope. We began with King's longing for 'a few, quiet English saints', men and women who would, without fuss or display or brashness, humbly press on with the ministry of the foot-washing and incarnate Christ's love for the world. He would urge his people to go quietly, bravely, steadily on in the living of the Christian life, and urge his confirmands, 'Be calm—nothing helps others more than a gentle calmness in this rough world.'[18] King was one of the quiet in the land, with a profound distaste for all that was loud and boastful and brash. He deplored what he called, in a brilliant piece of shorthand, 'tail-lashing' in the pulpit. The same dislike of brouhaha may underlie his confession that he 'liked missions, but not missioners . . .'. All this side of King must be set in the context of the Tractarian teaching on 'reserve' or restraint in imparting religious teaching. The communication of the Gospel must be proportioned to the needs and condition of the individual. The same battery of standard texts was not to be brought to bear upon all and sundry. Indeed, as David Newsome underlines, 'High Churchmen considered that the facile bandying of biblical texts was a debasing of scriptural truths into meaningless clichés: the endless repetition of pious injunctions could so easily degenerate into cant.'[19] In King's preference for 'quietness' as against much speaking, there may also have been an element of the countryman's ability to remain unimpressed by a display of fine words, unless they are backed by character and deeds. What Owen Chadwick says of Isaac Williams, as the type of the Tractarian country priest, expresses King's own attitude, and shows that it rests on the conviction that truth can prevail, without the benefit of a loud-hailer : 'In some ways the most "typical" figure of the whole movement is none of the leaders but Isaac Williams—pupil of Keble; poet; quiet and obscure country parson; avoiding noise and publicity and controversy (though he found it without intending to find it). The truth, Keble had taught the clergy, will not be popular . . . We must not expect more than a remnant of faithful men. We must expect criticism and even abuse, that is always the way of truth. And we must go about our parishes, quietly, diligently, unassertively, but faithful to our commission, leading our people into the community of Christ which is the Church, and therefore keeping from them nothing of that body of truth which the Church declares to us authoritatively, in such a manner as they are each able, in their moral and spiritual condition, to receive it'.[20] Subtract the tinge of pessimism from Keble's words, and you have King's viewpoint to a nicety.

The purging out of the pessimism which seems almost endemic in the earlier Tractarian tradition brings us to the note of joy in King. 'Brightness' was one of his favourite words in thinking of the Christian life; 'glowing' one of his characteristic adjectives. 'Serve the Lord with gladness' might be written over his whole Christian life.[21] Canon—later Bishop—Walsham How speaks of King's 'loving, beautiful brightness of manner'[22] when he gave a series of meditations in his parish in 1869. It was Pope Benedict XIV who laid down in his great book on canonization that in addition to the three traditional marks of sainthood—popular cultus, three miracles, three heroic acts—there should be a fourth : the note of joy. King had it remarkably— and in striking contrast to some of the great founding fathers of Tractarianism. Newman in his Anglican days could reply to criticism of the harshness of his first published sermons, 'We *require* the "Law's stern fires". We need a continual Ash Wednesday.'[23] The 'undercurrent of pessimism and gloom'[24] in the older Tractarians is clearly discernible in Pusey. After his wife's death, he became more and more the recluse, immured in his rooms in Christ Church, reading no newspapers, out of touch with modern trends even in his own scholarly field of study. Despite his chapped hands, he would not wear gloves in winter as a penitential discipline, and contemplated taking a vow not to smile until Keble talked him out of it. Small wonder that when Pusey died in 1882, York Powell, a lusty, beer-drinking, life-loving, pagan don at Christ Church, dismissed the great divine as 'this miserable little man' who had been one of 'the fighters against the light'.[25]

King was at the opposite pole from all that. He had an almost Franciscan joy in nature, and loved birds and trees and plants and flowers : 'All nature was to him a burning bush aflame with God.'[26] Only five years before he died, he preached—an old man of seventy-six—a great sermon of thanksgiving at the end of the typhoid epidemic in Lincoln in June 1905. 'I will thank Him', he proclaimed to his congregation in the cathedral, 'for the pleasures given me through my senses, for the glory of the thunder, for the mystery of music, the singing of birds and the laughter of children. I will thank him for the pleasures of seeing, for the delights through colour, for the awe of the sunset, the beauty of flowers, the smile of friendship and the look of love; for the changing beauty of the clouds, for the wild roses in the hedges, for the form and the beauty of birds, for the leaves on the trees in spring and autumn, for the witness of the leafless trees through the winter, teaching us that death is sleep and not destruction, for the sweetness of flowers and the scent of hay. Truly, O Lord, the earth is full of thy riches !'[27]

This joy in creation was simply an overflow of the joy which came from being committed in heart and life to God in Jesus Christ. 'In order to sew,' says Kierkegaard, 'we must have a knot in the thread.' King knew that once a man had that 'knot' of commitment, dedication, then his heart was set free : free for Christ, for others, for joy. A text he liked to quote was, 'My heart is fixed, therefore will I sing'. He longed for 'people who have the spirit of detachment, joy, and brightness'.[28] When he was nearly sixty-five, he wrote to a friend, 'What I hope rather to do now is (D.V.) to spend what remains in trying to understand what it means to be a Christian. I think it ought to ... make us restful, and hopefully happy, with a simple sense of freedom, and with a royal beauty and courage.'[29] 'Hopefully happy' just about describes his faith and life. In 1935, when the great service of commemoration was held for him in Lincoln Cathedral, a quarter-century after his death, the *Church Times* reporter went out into the High Street and talked to the local folk who remembered him as their bishop : 'For all them High Church doin's they had him up for', said one, 'he was niver a one for standing on ceremony. He'd go down the High Street of a market day and mix with the folks, an' have a joke with 'em too, for he wasn't above a joke. And how he loved the bairns.' One lady remembered him as 'a bit gay for a gospel preacher', but that was no typical complaint. The general verdict was rather, 'Whativer way you recollect him, you couldn't help but love him'.[30]

Part of the secret of King's appeal to all sorts and conditions of men, which the people who met him in Lincoln High Street knew, was the breadth of his sympathy. When King died in 1910, Francis Paget knew a 'great impoverishment' in his own life, and added : 'I doubt whether any one has left more hearts feeling the poorer for his death, or more lives the better for his life—for he was just the same to all sorts and conditions of men.'[31] Not, of course, that King meted out the same treatment to all sorts. How could he, granted the enormous diversity of human need? The point Paget is making is that King was unwavering in his attitude of concern and consideration for everyone he met. Hilaire Belloc made the point that 'The grace of God is in courtesy', and men observed in Edward King 'an enchanting courtesy'.[32] 'Socially he was amazing,' says F. E. Brightman 'he moved up and down the social strata without effort; or rather he seemed to have no sense of social distinctions, and could talk to everyone "in the language wherein he was born," so that the ploughboy could say he must have been a ploughboy himself. He was so absolutely a gentleman that his rustics could say there was nothing of the gentleman about him.'[33]

Belloc was right—the grace of God *is* in courtesy: in the consideration which is given to all, with 'undistinguishing regard'; and in the prevenience which takes the initiative and makes the first move in charity.

King's sympathy gave him an amazing insight and tact and delicacy in dealing with individuals in their need. He had a profound sense of respect for the integrity of the other person, whom he never sought to constrain or cajole. He once made a memorable speech to a large meeting of undergraduates in Christ Church hall, on his first appearance in Oxford after being consecrated Bishop of Lincoln. The meeting was held to raise support for Oxford House, Bethnal Green, one of the university missions and settlements in the East End. King had packed up his household ready for the move to Lincoln, and all he had left, he told them, was a Bible, a copy of Tertullian, and a match-box. He took his text for this occasion, not from the Bible nor from the early Church Father, but from the match-box, which in Victorian times carried the instruction, 'Rub lightly'. Father J. G. Adderley, the founder of Oxford House, heard the speech : 'It was a marvellous speech. We were to rub the East Enders—that is, we were to be definite, firm, sane, judicious; but we were to do it "lightly", with love and sympathy. We were not to make too much of the ecclesiastical "must"; but "just take them, and give them a little push—no more." The speech literally took us all by storm.'[34] King once wrote to a priest who had taken a new parish in the South of England, and was finding it rather hard going after the North : 'Everybody says the south people are much more difficult to rouse in matters of religion than the northern. But in time, please God, you will win them. You must go half steam, but with the full power of your love. They are shy, and meek, and afraid. Like fishing in the clear slow chalk streams of Hampshire, it requires very fine tackle and a delicate hand!'[35] What he longed for, both for himself and his clergy, was to be 'more kind, more considerate, less selfish even in carrying out religious plans, more ready to acknowledge God's Presence in others, and to fall in quietly and brightly with their different ways—freedom from any *religious harshness*, a docile, child-like, simple, loving spirit.'[36]

King recognized this quality of pastoral gentleness in his brother, Walker King, who died in 1893 after being Rector of St Clement's, Leigh-on-Sea, for thirty-three years. Edward preached his funeral sermon, on the text, 'Thy gentleness hath made me great' : 'In these days of self-advertisement and pushing, his spirit of gentleness and retirement possesses a rare value : always ready to listen to what other persons had to say; never over-bearing or pushing to obtain his own way, he would rather give way and let others do as they pleased, provided only it was not wrong.'[37] In a sermon preached towards the end of his life, at Lincoln in 1909, he traced this gentleness to its ultimate source in Christ : 'One of the most surprising marks of our Lord's words is their *gentleness*. He never exaggerates, never wishes to make people out worse than they are. He tries to think the best of people, and when He must point out their faults to warn them, He does it with a gentleness that no one could deny, or say that He has spoken too hardly, or not shown that gentleness is the absolute and awful truth.'[38]

King's simplicity should have already become apparent from what we have seen and heard of him : his simple speech and preaching style; his openness in personal relations and pastoral counselling; his humble manner of life as a minister. When he thanked his old Cuddesdon students for their presentation to him on his consecration, he said : 'The only thing is to see how we can be simple. I could see nothing else to do. All grows clear by taking God for our rest and end, with a sense of the reality of love and need of discipline. It gives a wonderful power of expansion, as the love of God and man is proved as a rule of life.'[39] For King the Christian life is fundamentally simple; not easy, or shallow, but simple; as simple and as profound as the truth that 'God is love'. The whole end and aim of life can be summed up in simple and unitary terms as 'the love of God and man', or 'faith working by love'. There was an evangelical dimension to his simplicity too, as he makes clear when he apologized to his men when he spoke to them for the last time

at his Friday evening 'Bethel' : 'I must ask pardon from you for
—I ought to say almost—my impudence in addressing you in
such simple language. But I have addressed you in this manner,
in order that you may be in strict communion with God; and
then that, through you, I might reach the poor.'[40] King's
simplicity is not naïve, childish, disingenuous. He has his eyes
wide open, and would endorse Von Hügel's belief that Christianity means 'Asceticism without Rigorism and Love without
Sentimentality'. It is the simplicity of the single eye, the one
thing needful, the pure in heart : the simplicity of Christ.

It is appropriate that we should close with King's quality of
hopefulness. He was always a 'hopefully happy' man, and a
spirit of humble hopefulness pervades his life and thought. So
many of the Tractarians had their gaze turned backwards to a
lost golden age—to the Church of the Caroline Divines or the
Middle Ages or the Early Fathers. King was concerned to 'guard
the deposit' and treasure the best of the past, but he had his face
turned to the future in hope. He had enormous faith in human
possibility, under the providence and grace of God. He did not,
like Liddon or Pusey, despair of the new age, much as he
deplored its materialism and unbelief. Teilhard de Chardin asks
in a letter of 1953, 'How is it possible that nine times out of ten
your believing Christian is at the human level a sceptic . . .?
This is what the Gentiles find so shocking.'[41] King would have
been shocked too, for he believed in the power of God in man
to transform and renew the world. His was an optimism of
grace. E. S. Talbot sensed his sympathy with the new age, his
willingness to move where it was right to move, and to serve as
mediator between old and new : 'His temperament radiated
sympathy, mental as well as moral and personal. He felt with
men, he felt with his time, he was conscious of the movement
under his feet. It did not carry him away, but there was appeal
in it; he felt the appeal, and responded to it. He wanted to learn
as well as to guide . . . he felt drawn to give younger men the
sympathy and help which can be given by one who, standing
between generations, can feel something of the new as well as the
old.'[42]

King gave a striking demonstration of his sympathy with a new generation, and with the thought of a new age, when in 1891 he invited Charles Gore to take the annual retreat for his clergy in Lincoln Cathedral. Gore was thirty-eight, and leader of the group of younger Anglo-Catholics who two years earlier had produced *Lux Mundi*, which set off the kind of furore in Victorian England which *Honest to God* aroused in the 1960s. Under the umbrella of their title, which pointed to Christ as the Light of the World, they tried creatively to come to terms with some of the new thought of their age. They shocked older High Churchmen by treating biblical criticism, evolutionary thought, and the political idealism of socialism, not as enemies of the gospel, but as potential channels of expression for the religion of the Incarnation. Gore, as editor of the book and author of the essay on 'Inspiration', was widely execrated. Liddon roundly condemned him as the betrayer of the legacy of Dr Pusey, and attempts were made to have him removed from the principalship of Pusey House, Oxford. In the midst of all this commotion, King deliberately invited Gore to Lincoln, to exercise a teaching ministry among his clergy. For one Tractarian bishop, at least, Gore's attempt at theological reconstruction in the light of the new thinking was no betrayal. Let King's forward-looking spirit have the last word. In 1873, he wrote to an old student, just beginning his parish ministry : 'There is a very great opportunity for you. I am sure we must be full of hope—brave, self-sacrificing, victorious hope. To me, thank God, all these troubles of the intellect, and all our ecclesiastical and social anxieties, are full of hope. They are but, I believe, the pain and labour which will issue in the birth of more truth, more true liberty, more true union between man and nature, and man and God, a bringing us in all things nearer to *Him*. Only, dearest child, in all this we must keep quiet and steady in our personal union with Him.'[43]

Epilogue

> Saints are the popular evidence of Christianity. The life of a saint is a microcosm or whole work of God, a perfect work from beginning to end, yet one which may be bound between two boards and mastered by the most unlearned.
>
> *John Henry Newman*

IN our end is our beginning.... We started out in this search with Edward King's longing, 'to write some 2d Lives of English Saints, with the names of counties and parishes and people we know, so that others may read them and try to do the same. Do let us try and rear a few quiet English saints!' We can only regret that King never produced his twopenny lives of home-grown, quiet English saints. They would doubtless have been gems, as free from conventional hagiography as his own life was from religiosity. The economics of publishing have put paid to the idea of twopenny Lives, but we still need what King was after, and there is a rich seam to be worked.

He did manage to produce one life of a quiet English saint, though. It could not be bound between two boards while he lived, but it can now: the life of Edward King. He was widely recognized as a saint in his lifetime, the impress of his holiness felt by wise and simple alike. 'Do they always send a saint from Heaven to confirm you and does he go back into Heaven?' a boy asked his mother after King had bent to bless him in con-firmation. The sixty-seven years that have passed since King's death have abundantly confirmed that judgement. His memory in Lincolnshire and far beyond is evergreen; the tradition of his words and deeds is alive and fruitful; the fellowship of his spirit in the Communion of Saints is known and realized as a blessing. Men and women who never knew him in the flesh, as well as those happy few still alive who did, kindle at his name; for they recognize him as a living witness to the power of Christ's grace and love.

To his own favourite text, 'Thy gentleness hath made me great', we may add two more, both of a piece with it, which are carved on the plinth of his statue in Lincoln Cathedral : 'Beloved, let us love one another, for love is of God'; and 'Blessed are the meek, for they shall inherit the earth'. At Cuddesdon, where he knew a happiness so deep as to be a foretaste of heaven, he is commemorated with a special warmth of thanksgiving. The collect prescribed for his day—8 March, the anniversary of his death—conveys the quintessence of this quiet English saint : 'O Almighty God, who gavest such grace unto thy servant Edward King that whomsoever he met, he drew nearer unto thee; Fill us, we beseech thee, with sympathy as tender and deep, that we also may win others to know the love which passeth knowledge; through Jesus Christ thy Son our Lord. Amen.'

Notes

Chapter One: Search for a Saint

1. A. M. Allchin in M. Chavchavadze, ed., *Man's Concern with Holiness* (1970), p.37
2. J. G. Lockhart, *Cosmo Gordon Lang* (1949), p.66.
3. B. W. Randolph and J. W. Townroe, *The Mind and Work of Bishop King* (1918), pp.9–10 (afterwards referred to as 'Randolph and Townroe').
4. A Souvenir of the Sexcentenary Celebrations of the Foundation Stone Laying of St Botolph's, Boston. 1309–1909. Reprinted from the *Boston Guardian* (1909), p.40.
5. *Ibid.*
6. *The Tablet*, 4 January 1975, p.7.
7. Randolph and Townroe, p.7.
8. H. Scott Holland, *A Bundle of Memories* (1915), p.48.
9. Cecilia M. Ady, *The English Church and how it works* (1940), p.218.
10. Lincolnshire Archives (afterwards 'L.A.'), Larken IV/1. f.1.
11. L. A., Larken IV/1. ff.3-21.
12. Edward King, *The Love and Wisdom of God*, ed. B. W. Randolph (1910), p.180.
13. *Ibid.*, pp.184–5.
14. *Spiritual Letters of Edward King, D.D.*, ed. B. W. Randolph (1910), p.44 (afterwards, *Spiritual Letters*).
15. W. Tuckwell, *Reminiscences of Oxford* (2nd Edn. 1907), p.143.
16. Quoted in John Coulson, A. M. Allchin, and M. Trevor, *Newman: A Portrait Restored* (1965), p.21.
17. Edward King, *The Love and Wisdom of God*, p.132.
18. *Spiritual Letters*, p.35.

Chapter Two: The Oriel Undergraduate

1. Edward King, *Meditations on the Last Seven Words of our Lord Jesus Christ* (1910), p.2.
2. Edward King, *Sermons and Addresses* (1911), pp.73–4.
3. G. W. E. Russell, *Edward King Sixtieth Bishop of Lincoln* (1912), p.3. (Afterwards, 'Russell').
4. Russell, p.114.
5. Tuckwell, *Reminiscences of Oxford*, p.180.
6. See Randolph and Townroe, p.24.
7. *Spiritual Letters*, pp.10–11.
8. Russell, p.6.
9. Russell, *loc. cit.*
10. *Spiritual Letters*, p.11.

11. Russell, pp.6, 350.
12. Russell, p.5.
13. Tuckwell, *Reminiscences of Oxford*, pp.187–8.
14. O. Chadwick, *The Founding of Cuddesdon* (1954), pp.150–1.
15. Tuckwell, *Reminiscences of Oxford*, p.189. See also R. W. Church, *The Oxford Movement: Twelve Years 1833–1845* (3rd edn. 1892), p.84.
16. R. W. Church, *The Oxford Movement*, pp.87–8.
17. Russell, p.5.
18. Edward King, *The Love and Wisdom of God*, p.320.
19. Tuckwell, *Reminiscences of Oxford*, p.190.

Chapter Three: Cuddesdon
1. *Letters of C. S. Lewis*, ed. W. H. Lewis (1966), p.60.
2. *Correspondence on Church and Religion of William Ewart Gladstone*, ed. D. C. Lathbury, 2 vols. (1910), I, 210.
3. Chadwick, *Founding of Cuddesdon*, pp.16–17.
4. D. MacLeane, *A History of Pembroke College, Oxford* (1897), p.460n.
5. J. W. Mackail, *The Life of William Morris* (1899), in Oxford World's Classics edn. (1950), p.87.
6. V. H. H. Green, *Religion at Oxford and Cambridge* (1964), p.365.
7. Chadwick, *Founding of Cuddesdon*, p.7.
8. *Ibid.*, p.8.
9. G. F. A. Best, 'Popular Protestantism in Victorian Britain', in *Ideas and Institutions of Victorian Britain*, ed. R. Robson (1967), p.124.
10. *Rambler*, July 1860; printed in *Letters and Diaries of John Henry Newman*, ed. C. S. Dessain, XIX (1969), 551.
11. Quoted in Chadwick, *Founding of Cuddesdon*, p.25.
12. A. R. Ashwell and R. G. Wilberforce, *The Life of the Right Reverend Samuel Wilberforce, D.D.*, 3 vols. (1880–82), II, 359.
13. See Lee's account of his own relations with Liddon in H.R.T. Brandreth, *Dr. Lee of Lambeth* (1952), p.8. For Lee see also Chadwick, *Founding of Cuddesdon*, p.61.
14. Chadwick, *Founding of Cuddesdon*, p.151.
15. *Ibid.*, p.101.
16. *Ibid.*, p.80.
17. Ashwell and Wilberforce, *Life of Samuel Wilberforce*, II, 367–8.

Chapter Four: Principal King
1. Randolph and Townroe, p.41.
2. Chadwick, *Founding of Cuddesdon*, pp.84–5.
3. *Ibid.*, p.88.
4. *Cuddesdon College 1854–1904: a record and memorial* (1904), pp.51–2 (afterwards, *Cuddesdon College*).
5. Chadwick, *Founding of Cuddesdon*, p.153.
6. *Cuddesdon College*, pp.119–20.
7. *Ibid.*, p.119.
8. *Ibid.*, p.67.

9. *Spiritual Letters*, pp.22–3.
10. G. F. Wilgress, *Edward King, Bishop of Lincoln, 1885–1910* (no date), pp.8–9.
11. Randolph and Townroe, p.46.
12. *Ibid.*, p.47.
13. Wilgress, *Edward King*, p.8.
14. Chadwick, *Founding of Cuddesdon*, p.94.
15. Randolph and Townroe, p.53.
16. *Spiritual Letters*, p.104.
17. See above, pp.37–8.
18. Lord Elton, *Edward King and our times* (1958), p.52 (afterwards, Elton, *Edward King*).
19. Charles Smyth, *The Church and the Nation* (1962), p.171.
20. Randolph and Townroe, p.14.
21. C. J. Smith, *Berkeley William Randolph: A Memoir* (1925), p.58.
22. *Pastoral Lectures of Bishop Edward King*, ed. Eric Graham (1932), pp.20–1 (afterwards, *Pastoral Lectures*).
23. Elton, *Edward King*, p.54.
24. *A Forty Years' Friendship: Letters from the late Henry Scott Holland to Mrs. Drew*, ed. S. L. Ollard (1919), p.97.
25. *Spiritual Letters*, p.183.
26. *Ibid.*, p.111.
27. H. S. Holland, *A Bundle of Memories*, p.51.
28. F. H. West, *Sparrows of the Spirit* (1961), p.113.
29. Russell, p.107.
30. *Cuddesdon College*, p.52.

Chapter Five: The Pastoral Professor

1. H. P. Liddon, *Life of Edward Bouverie Pusey*, 4 vols. (1893–97), IV, 221.
2. Russell, p.39.
3. Edward King, *The Love and Wisdom of God*, p.134. See also Russell, p.38.
4. O. Chadwick, *Edward King, Bishop of Lincoln 1885–1910*, Lincoln Minster Pamphlets, 2nd series, No.4. (1968), p.7. (Tait to Gladstone, 24 February 1873).
5. R. T. Davidson and W. Benham, *Life of Archibald Campbell Tait*, 2 vols. (1891), II, 524.
6. Russell, p.107.
7. Russell, p.38.
8. Randolph and Townroe, p.81.
9. Russell, p.51.
10. Chadwick, *Edward King*, p.8.
11. F. E. Brightman's article on 'Edward King', in *A Dictionary of English Church History*, edd. S. L. Ollard and G. Crosse (1912), p.308.
12. Randolph and Townroe, pp.79–80.
13. *Ibid.*, p.136.

14. A. Pütz, 'Bischof Edward King, ein anglikanischer Sailerfreund', in *Kurtrierisches Jahrbuch* (1968), pp.291–9.
15. A. T. P. Williams' article in *Dictionary of National Biography, 1931–1940*, s.v. 'Charles Gore'.
16. W. H. Hutton, obituary notice of Edward King in the *Church Family Newspaper* for March 1910.
17. Published by Mowbray, this small 78–page paperback volume, despite its relatively recent date, is extremely hard to come by.
18. Randolph and Townroe, p.84.
19. W. H. Hutton in *Church Family Newspaper*, March 1910.
20. *Pastoral Lectures*, p.15.
21. *Ibid.*, p.7.
22. *Ibid.*, p.12.
23. Chadwick, *Edward King*, p.9. Cf. K. E. Kirk, *Some Principles of Moral Theology and their application* (1920), p. 8n.,–' "Read the Bible, the *Ethics*, and good novels," is said to have been Bishop King's advice to inquirers who wished for guidance in the study of moral theology.'
24. *Pastoral Lectures*, p.32.
25. Randolph and Townroe, p.75.
26. K. E. Kirk, *Some Principles of Moral Theology*, p.8.
27. S. Paget and J. C. M. Crum, *Francis Paget* (1912), p.12.
28. Randolph and Townroe, pp.10–11.
29. Paget and Crum, *Francis Paget*, p.30.
30. Randolph and Townroe, p.52.
31. *Pastoral Lectures*, p.5.
32. *Ibid.*, p.8.,
33. Chadwick, *Edward King*, p.9.
34. Russell, p.59.
35. Chadwick, *Edward King*, p.11.
36. *A Forty Years' Friendship,* ed. Ollard, p.37.
37. Russell, p.98.
38. *The Letters of A. E. Housman,* ed. Henry Maas (1971), p.17.
39. 'Q' (Sir Arther Quiller-Couch), *Memories and Opinions: An unfinished autobiography,* ed. S. C. Roberts (1944), pp.54–5.
40. Randolph and Townroe, p.54.
41. *Ibid.*, pp.6–7.
42. *Ibid.*, p.53.
43. *The Life and Work of John Richardson Illingworth,* ed. by his Wife (1917), p.6.
44. Russell, p.96.
45. *Spiritual Letters,* p.116, and see also p.24 for his thinking of work in Australia.
46. *The Silent Rebellion* (1958), p.240.
47. Cuddesdon College, p.128.
48. C. P. S. Clarke, *The Oxford Movement and After* (1932), pp.246–7.
49. C. E. Mallett, *A History of the University of Oxford,* 3 vols. (1924–27), III, 432n.

50. Edward King, *The Love and Wisdom of God*, p.156.
51. *Ibid.*, p.168.

Chapter Six: Lincoln: 'A Bishop of the Poor'
1. *Spiritual Letters*, p.146.
2. *Ibid.*, pp.23–4.
3. *Ibid.*, p.54.
4. See Chadwick, *Edward King*, p.10.
5. Chadwick, *Edward King*, p.12.
6. Russell, p.86.
7. *Ibid.*, p.87.
8. G. L. Prestige, *The Life of Charles Gore* (1935), p.76.
9. Russell, pp.92–3.
10. Russell, p.90.
11. *A Forty Years' Friendship*, ed. Ollard, p.86.
12. *A Forty Years' Friendship*, ed. Ollard, p.97.
13. Russell, p.93.
14. *Ibid.*, p.96.
15. *Ibid.*, p.103.
16. Chadwick, *Edward King*, p.14.
17. Russell, pp.104–5.
18. 'Q', *Memories and Opinions*, p.26.
19. Chadwick, *Edward King*, p.16.
20. *Church Times*, 24 May 1935.
21. Russell, p.212.
22. *Proceedings of the Second Ecumenical Methodist Conference* (1892), pp.125–6.
23. *Spiritual Letters*, p.184.
24. *Ibid.*, p.108.
25. Russell, p.145.
26. *Methodist Recorder*, 22 July 1909, p.4.
27. Russell, p.86.
28. Randolph and Townroe, p.231.
29. Russell, p.96.
30. For the oral source of this quotation, see above, p.4.
31. W. Addison, *The English Country Parson* (1947), pp.188–9.
32. Russell, p.108.
33. *Ibid.*, pp.94–5.
34. Edward King, *Sermons and Addresses*, p.162.
35. *Ibid.*, pp.25–6.
36. Bodleian Library, Oxford. Wilberforce Papers. Letter of King to Wilberforce, 26 December 1866.
37. G. Shaw, *Our Religious Humorists* (1880), p.225.
38. J. C. Hardwick, *Lawn Sleeves: A Short Life of Samuel Wilberforce* (1933), p.189.
39. *Lincolnshire Life*, July 1968, Vol. 8. No. 5, p.31.
40. Russell, p.124.
41. *Ibid.*, pp.125–6.

42. *Ibid.*, p.127.

Chapter Seven: Bishop on Trial
 1. Bodleian Library, Western MSS., St Edmund Hall, 64f. 55v.
 2. E. K. Paget, *H. L. Paget*, pp.57–8.
 3. Chadwick, *Edward King*, p.18.
 4. *Ibid.*, p.19.
 5. C. J. Smith, *B. W. Randolph*, p.37.
 6. Russell, pp.176–7.
 7. *Ibid.*, pp.166–7.
 8. *The Life and Letters of Dean Church*, ed. Mary Church (1897), p.421.
 9. Russell, pp.198–9.
10. L. A., Larken III/59.
11. Chadwick, *Edward King*, p.18.
12. L. A., Larken III/17.
13. Russell, p.210.

Chapter Eight: 'Thy gentleness hath made me great'
 1. *The Spiritual Maxims of St. Francis de Sales*, ed. C. F. Kelley (1954), p.124.
 2. Pope John XXIII, *Journal of a Soul* (1965), pp.268, 283–4.
 3. Martin Thornton, *English Spirituality* (1963), p.14.
 4. See Thornton, *English Spirituality*, pp.46, 50–1, 83.
 5. A. M. Allchin in Chavchavadze, *Man's Concern with Holiness*, p.46.
 6. Edward King, *The Love and Wisdom of God*, p.138.
 7. Scott Holland, *A Bundle of Memories*, pp.49–50.
 8. Chadwick, *Founding of Cuddesdon*, p.112.
 9. E. K. Paget, *Henry Luke Paget* (1939), pp.109–10.
10. Bramwell Booth, *Echoes and Memories* (1925), p.74.
11. B. L. Manning, *The Hymns of Wesley and Watts* (1942), p.133.
12. *Ibid.*, pp.132–3; *Methodist Hymn Book*, No. 368.
13. *Unity Begins at Home:* a report from the first British Conference on Faith and Order, Nottingham 1964 (1964), p.29.
14. H. E. Sheen, *Canon Peter Green* (1965), p.35.
15. Edward King, *Sermons and Addresses*, p.118.
16. Edward King, *Personal and Parochial* (1912), p.45.
17. Paget and Crum, *Francis Paget*, p.104.
18. Edward King, *Sermons and Addresses*, p.156.
19. D. Newsome, *The Parting of Friends: a study of the Wilberforces and Henry Manning* (1966), p.74.
20. O. Chadwick, *The Mind of the Oxford Movement* (1960), p.35.
21. Randolph and Townroe, p.8.
22. F. D. How, *Bishop Walsham How: A Memoir* (1898), p.96.
23. Quoted in *The Rediscovery of Newman: An Oxford Symposium*, ed. J. Coulson and A. M. Allchin (1967), p.25.
24. Newsome, *Parting of Friends*, p.180.
25. O. Elton, *Frederick York Powell: A Life*, 2 vols. (1906), I, 66–67.
26. Randolph and Townroe, p.11.

27. Edward King, *Sermons and Addresses*, pp.37–8.
28. *Ibid.*, p.59.
29. *Spiritual Letters*, p.178.
30. *Church Times*, 24 May 1935.
31. Paget and Crum, *Francis Paget*, p.321.
32. Chadwick, *Edward King*, p.3.
33. Brightman on King, in Ollard and Crosse, *Dictionary of English Church History*, p.308.
34. Russell, p.110.
35. *Spiritual Letters*, p.59.
36. *Ibid.*, p.42.
37. Edward King, *The Love and Wisdom of God*, p.278.
38. Edward King, *Sermons and Addresses*, pp.78–9.
39. Russell, p.108.
40. *Ibid.*, p.99.
41. Quoted in N. M. Wildiers, *An Introduction to Teilhard de Chardin* (Fontana edn. 1968), p.118.
42. Randolph and Townroe, p.86.
43. *Spiritual Letters*, p.33.

BOOKS FOR FURTHER READING

Works of Edward King

Spiritual Letters of Edward King, D.D., ed. B. W. Randolph, (A. R. Mowbray), 1910.
The Love and Wisdom of God: being a collection of sermons, ed. B. W. Randolph, (Longmans), 1910.
Sermons and Addresses, ed. B. W. Randolph, (Longmans), 1911.
Pastoral Lectures of Bishop Edward King, ed. Eric Graham, (A. R. Mowbray), 1932.

Studies of Edward King
CHADWICK, O., *Edward King Bishop of Lincoln 1885–1910*, Lincoln Minister Pamphlets Second Series No. 4 (Friends of Lincoln Cathedral), 1968.
ELTON, Lord, *Edward King and Our Times*, (Bles), 1958.
RANDOLPH, B. W. and TOWNROE, J. W., *The Mind and Work of Bishop King*, (A. R. Mowbray), 1918.
RUSSELL, G. W. E., *Edward King Sixtieth Bishop of Lincoln: A Memoir*, (Smith, Elder & Co.), 1912.
WILGRESS, G. F., *Edward King Bishop of Lincoln*, (Bishop of Lincoln's Appeal Fund), n.d.

Index